The Ultimate Investment Guide

Learn How to Invest Like the Pros. Gain Financial Independence Through Savvy Investing

Nicolas Leonard

© Copyright 2020 by Nicolas Leonard. All right reserved.

The work contained herein has been produced with the intent to provide relevant knowledge and information on the topic on the topic described in the title for entertainment purposes only. While the author has gone to every extent to furnish up to date and true information, no claims can be made as to its accuracy or validity as the author has made no claims to be an expert on this topic. Notwithstanding, the reader is asked to do their own research and consult any subject matter experts they deem necessary to ensure the quality and accuracy of the material presented herein.

This statement is legally binding as deemed by the Committee of Publishers Association and the American Bar Association for the territory of the United States. Other jurisdictions may apply their own legal statutes. Any reproduction, transmission or copying of this material contained in this work without the express written consent of the copyright holder shall be deemed as a copyright violation as per the current legislation in force on the date of publishing and subsequent time thereafter. All additional works derived from this material may be claimed by the holder of this copyright.

The data, depictions, events, descriptions and all other information forthwith are considered to be true, fair and accurate unless the work is expressly described as a work of fiction. Regardless of the nature of this work, the Publisher is exempt from any responsibility of actions taken by the reader in conjunction with this work. The Publisher acknowledges that the reader acts of their own accord and releases the author and Publisher of any responsibility for the observance of tips, advice, counsel, strategies and techniques that may be offered in this volume.

Table of Contents

Introduction 6
Chapter 1: Becoming an Investor - The Most Important Decision of Your Life 9

   Making the Decision to Become an Investor 10
   How to Get Started 12
   Cutting Out Money Wasters From Your Life 15
   Saving = Investment 17
   Become an Investor and Not Just a Consumer 19
   Setting the Right Objectives 23

Chapter 2: Learning the Rules of Investing 27

   All About Financial Assets 28
   Passive and Active Investing Through ETFs 38
   Golden Rules of Money Management 40
   Mistakes to Avoid as a New Investor 42

Chapter 3: Low-Cost Investments to Make Your Portfolio Grow 45

   The Cost Associated With Investments 47
   Membership Fees 48
   Commissions 49
   Taxes 50
   How to Make Money From Various Investments 52
   Profiting From ETFs 56
   How ETFs Make Money 57
   Tips and Strategies for Investing in ETFs 59

Chapter 4: Investing in Cryptocurrencies 62

Fundamentals of Cryptocurrencies 64
How to Invest in Cryptos 67
Rules for Investing in Cryptos 71
Mistakes to Watch Out for When Investing in Cryptos 76

Chapter 5: Making the Right Investment Decisions 80

Converting Dividends Into Income 82
Proper Asset Allocation Based on Age 86
Diversification as a Means of Balancing Risk in Your Portfolio 90
Passive Income From Investing 93
Automating Investments 95

Chapter 6: Knowledge Is Not Power… Action Is! 97

The First Steps You Can Take as a New Investor 99
How to Have Fun While Making Money 103
Seeking Other More Experienced Investors 105
Looking Toward the Future of Investing 108
The Name of the Game Is "Flexibility" 110

Conclusion 113

Introduction

Welcome to, "The Ultimate Investment Guide: Learn How to Invest Like the Pros. Gain financial independence through savvy investing". Thank you very much for taking the time to read this book. This volume will surely become your go-to guide for all things related to investing and financial matters.

In the following pages, you will find a trove of information that has been distilled from years of experience and study. As a result, years of experience and training have been condensed into an easy-to-follow guide which will provide you with everything you need to know about the world of investing.

If you are new to the investment world, then we hope that you will feel confident in your ability to make money by the time you're done with this book. We have taken great care to provide you with all of the tools and knowledge you need in order to figure out the best plan based on your personal goals and needs.

If you are an experienced investor, we hope that the knowledge and information in this book will complement what you have already learned throughout your time in the investing world. Best of all, you won't find any esoteric jargon in this book. We have ensured that this book tells things the way they are. So, you won't have to scratch your head at the fancy language used to sound smart.

Each of the sections in this book has been designed to deal with a core element of investing. Consequently, you'll find that each chapter covers vital information that all investors need to know. Most importantly, we'll be covering aspects that you might not have paid closer attention to in the past. After all, understanding the world of investing is a matter of knowledge and experience.

We will be discussing the various elements that are needed to become a successful investor. However, you won't find any magic formulas here. Everything we will be discussing is the result of time-tested techniques that real investors have tried out. This means that you can be sure that you're getting the real deal here. There are no gimmicks and no false promises. Everything you will find here is the results of dedicated work and research.

So, what do you have to lose?

Nothing!

When you apply the principles, practices, and experiences we have outlined throughout this book; you'll become cognizant of the best ways to invest your money while also avoiding the pitfalls that can derail your plans. In following the proper guidelines, you will discover the best path to your particular goals and ambitions.

Please keep in mind that this goes beyond simply making money. This is about taking these concepts and building a carefully designed approach that will lead you to become successful in the long run. Ultimately, you won't have to second guess any of your decisions. You'll feel confident that you have made the best possible decision based on the data you have available.

So, come on! Let's get started on the road that leads to financial independence.

Chapter 1: Becoming an Investor - The Most Important Decision of Your Life

Becoming an investor is not a decision to be made lightly. Sure, you hear folks talk about investing money in the stock market. You may hear others say they have money invested in the "market." What most folks don't realize is that investing in a mutual fund or a 401(k) isn't quite "investing in the market."

You see, when you purchase a mutual fund or put money into your 401(k), what you are really doing is giving your money to a professional money manager. This money manager then decides to allocate it in whatever investments they feel are the most appropriate for them.

Please keep this in mind.

Professional managers are only thinking about making their bosses happy and padding their bonuses. From the profits they make, retail customers get their cut. This is why you hear investment advisors tell you that you need to have a long-term approach. Moreover, they tell you that you need to ride out bear markets and focus on the "big picture."

The are catchphrases that investment managers use to convince their clients that you can make money by investing over decades as opposed to making decent returns in a shorter period of time. This is why you need to take control of your investment decisions. That way, even if you decide to hire a money manager, you can tell them exactly what kind of investments you are looking to make.

In addition, when you are well versed in investment matters, you will fully understand the options that are around you. That way, you won't base your retirement solely on the value of your 401(k). If anything, your 401(k) or mutual funds will serve as one source of income for you down the road.

That's why this chapter is focused on making the decision to become an investor. We will discuss what it means to "invest" and what you can expect from investing.

Making the Decision to Become an Investor

It should be said that becoming an investor isn't for everyone. Learning about the various types of investments, their valuation, returns, and keeping up with the latest investment information isn't something that most folks want to do. In fact, most folks dream of just putting money into an account and suddenly making a profit.

Mutual funds and 401(k)s were created for folks like this. These are passive investment vehicles that don't require the investor to do anything beyond fund their account. It should also be noted that they are extremely risky as their valuation is based on the current market valuation.

Consider this situation:

You put down $100 into a mutual fund. This money buys you 10 shares of TRG corp. Each share is valued at $10 apiece. Now, let's say that TRG publishes highly successful results for the year. So, the stock climbs to $12 a share. Your portfolio is now worth $120. That's a 20% jump. If you cashed out at that point, you would make a 20% profit. Now consider the opposite scenario. TRG Corp tanks. Shares plummet from $10 to $5 a share. All of a sudden, you have taken a 50% haircut.

This is why investing in mutual funds and 401(k)s can be highly risky. When you decide to call up your broker and ask them about your account, the only thing they will tell you is that you need to ride it out. The market will come back, and you'll end up making more money than you did before.

Had you been on top of the markets, you could have called up your broker at the first sign of trouble and asked them to liquidate your position. You may have to pay a penalty for cashing out, but then again, you wouldn't have lost half of your portfolio.

Then again, if you are a passive investor, you really have no choice but to ride out the market. Hopefully, you'll be able to make your money back, and then some, by the time you actually need it, say, around the time you're ready to retire.

So, if you're ready to take control of your investments, even if you don't actively trade in anything, then read on. You'll be so glad you took control of your portfolio the next time the market takes a downturn. By being aware of the market and the current situation, you could save yourself from financial disaster.

How to Get Started

Getting started as an investor is a lot easier than you think. The first big decision you need to make is whether you want to be an active or passive investor. This is a key decision as your choice of being active or passive will determine how much time and effort you need to put into studying and understanding the world of investing.

As we have stated earlier, if you are not keen on taking on a more active role, then it would be best for you to find a reputable broker or financial institution. Then, purchase one of their most popular products, such as a mutual fund, index fund, or high yield investment account. Once you have that setup, you can then go about putting money into that fund every month. When you sign your contract, make sure you read the

fine print. It will say that your broker has the authority to make investment decisions on your behalf without the need to consult your opinion. This is important as it essentially means they can do whatever they want with your money.
That being said, let's take a look at how you can become an active investor without having to quit your day job.

First of all, let's look at working a broker or hiring a professional money manager. There are plenty of banks and other financial institutions out there that offer investment services. They offer investment advice and money management services. Since you are not planning on being a passive investor, you need to work with your broker so that they keep you in the loop about everything that's happening with your portfolio. Money managers are generally more willing to accommodate the wishes of high net worth individuals. These are "rich" investors who are willing to invest thousands, if not millions, into a single account.

There are many funds and banks out there with varying degrees of requirement. Rich investors' funds may require you to have a net worth of $5M. Some may ask you for an even higher net worth. Then, there are other funds that set the bar a little lower. Please search around for these types of funds as they are far more willing to work with individual investors as opposed to simply taking your money and sending you a statement at the end of the month.

If possible, try to avoid commercial banks. They offer low-interest rates and don't particularly cater to individual investors. They would just rather take your money and trade it themselves. They are not keen on getting any kind of input from their customers. As such, these types of schemes are more suited to passive investors.

When you talk to brokers, please make sure you go over the products they offer and the various options they have according to your net worth and investment capital. Please ensure that the contract you sign states that you have control over your account and can liquidate your position at any time without penalties.

This is the biggest loophole that investment firms use to lock in their customers.

You see, firms stipulate that you must remain in the fund X amount of time. If you choose to leave early, you will be penalized. This is why you need to hold on to 401(k)s until you retire. If you cash it in early, you have to pay fees and taxes.

Do you see why you need to have control over your investments?

So, do make sure that your broker can answer these questions and give you the opportunity to call them up to get your money back whenever you want it. In the event of an emergency, this can be your lifeline to your savings and investments.

Cutting Out Money Wasters From Your Life

One of the core tenets of investors is to be careful with their money. The old adage "no one become rich by spending money" rings truer than ever.

Now, we're not saying that you need to become a miser. What we are saying is that you need to be very careful with the way you spend your money. So, getting rid of money wasters is an essential part of the investment mindset. When you get rid of these wasters, you can then devote those funds to invest in. That's where profits really begin to pile up. In fact, you'll be so surprised how easy it is to build up your investment capital.

Some of the most common money wasters are fees. Yes, that's right, fees.

In practically all financial advice literature, you hear about how picking up a coffee every day is such a waste of money. You also get bogus advice about cutting your cable and downsizing your home. Sure, these all make sense if you are in way over your head. But the fact of the matter is that you waste a significant amount of money paying late fees on credit cards, interest on debt while racking up ATM fees. These fees tend to add up to hundreds, if not thousands, of dollars every year.

You can avoid these fees by being careful about your financial matters.

For instance, make sure you are fully aware of the payment date on your credit card. That way, you can pay on time and avoid the late fees. Likewise, making an effort to pay as much as you can on your card will keep you from accruing interest on it. If you can't make the full payment, then try your best to make more than the minimum payment.

If you are stuck with debt, please bear in mind that not all debt is bad. Of course, if you are bogged down by consumer debt, then you need to resolve to cut it out completely. At first, you may not save any money, but just being able to cut down on debt will enable you to devote funds to invest.

As for ATM fees, make sure that you know where you can make free withdrawals. Check with your bank to see which ATMs will not charge you any transaction fees. Avoiding these fees will go a long way. In addition, make sure that you are not getting nailed with maintenance fees on your bank account. It could be that you are unaware of monthly service charges for your account. If this is the case, then you need to find an account that won't charge you a service and/or has a lower minimum account balance.

Lastly, make sure that you avoid spending on needless items. While some impulse shopping can be fun (especially if you are surfing late at night), it's important to note that every you spend on something you don't need, you are letting your goals get further and further ahead. Always ask yourself, "do I really need this?" before spending. Of course, there are times when you can afford a luxury. But until you can comfortably afford such luxuries, you might want to avoid spending on items that don't necessarily add value to your life.

Saving = Investment

This formula is part of the core tenet of all successful investors. The reasoning behind this is that you cannot invest money you don't have. Sure, you could borrow money to invest. However, that wouldn't make any sense as the potential return you'd get on it would not make up for the interest you'd pay, at least not in the short term.

This means that saving money is all about having the funds to invest. Now, not all investments are related to stocks or financial assets. A worthwhile investment could be a rental property. Also, you could be looking at other types of assets, such as gold or cryptocurrency. The fact of the matter is that you don't necessarily have to invest in stocks or bonds.

Whatever you ultimately decide to invest in requires you to have money available. The only way you can be sure that you'll have the money to do so is to save as much as you can. It should be said that contrary to what most people believe, you don't need to have thousands of dollars to start investing. You can start investing with as little as $20. For instance, you could buy a one-ounce silver coin. While it may seem simple, but that's a start.

To make headway with your savings, it's good to have a plan. This plan should be a combination of realistic aims and reasonable efforts. For example, you could decide to save 20% of your income next month. But if you are living paycheck to paycheck, that might not be possible. However, you could say to yourself, "I can realistically save $50 next month". Even with $50, you are saving something. And that something is better than nothing at all.

So, let's do some math. If you choose to save $50 a month, you would be able to accumulate $300 over six months. That might not seem like a lot, but it would be enough for you to open up a mutual fund account. It would also be enough to get you into a stock index fund. Soon, your $300 will begin to accrue interest and increase in value. Again, you can't expect $300 to turn into $3,000 in a matter of weeks, but what you are doing is building healthy habits that will ensure you make the best possible profit at this point in your life.

The next step is to set up an emergency fund. Ideally, your emergency fund should cover at least six weeks of living expenses, including 1 to 2 months of rent or mortgage payments. This is important in case you lose your job or get sick. Additionally, it's a good cushion to have in case; heaven forbid, you should have a sudden illness in your family.

To set up the target fund, calculate your average weekly living expenses, and multiply that by 6. You should only include bare necessities, as anything beyond food, rent, insurance payments, and medication is practically a luxury.

As you build up your emergency fund, try your best to set a certain amount of your savings toward investing. This is what the term "pay yourself first" refers to. When you "pay yourself first," it means that you are setting money aside for your investment purposes. These funds will then pay off down the road. Hence, you are making an allowance for your future self.

As you get into the habit of saving, it's important to keep your eyes and ears open for investment opportunities, and no, we don't mean investing in your buddy's brand-new business. This is about finding reasonable investments, which you are sure can deliver you some kind of value at some point in the future.

Become an Investor and Not Just a Consumer

We are all consumers. We all purchase items that we need for our regular consumption. This is just a normal part of life. However, there are many folks out there who are nothing more than just consumers. They go about their lives consuming goods without making any provisions for their real needs.

Consider this situation:

A car is a means of transportation. In essence, all you really need is a car that can take you from point A to point B comfortably and safely. Under that premise, virtually any car in good condition would fit the bill.

So, does that mean that you need to purchase a new car?

No.

While some may argue that a new car provides them with the assurance that it is in good condition, the fact is that it is not absolutely necessary for a car to be brand new. This is also important when you consider the sticker price on a brand-new car. Therefore, you need to evaluate your real needs.

The pure consumer would do whatever they could to acquire the most expensive car they could. In their minds, this enables them to get bragging rights. The savvy investor would think twice about it. The savvy investor would like for the best price-to-value relation. This relation generally means finding a good, used automobile at a good price. After all, the only thing you need is a reliable means of transportation.

This example underscores the fact that you need you to think about value over price or appearance. When this occurs, you are able to make the most of your decisions. If you are willing to make certain trade-offs, then you will find that your money goes a lot further than you could have anticipated.

Additionally, putting the consumer mindset behind you leads to wiser financial choices. This is where investing comes in. When you decide to make wiser allocations of our money, you are able to find the means to really put your money to work for you. Thus, your money slowly begins to snowball.

As you begin to forget about buying new consumer electronics, trading in your car, or upgrading to a bigger house, you'll find that opportunities for growth are everywhere. You are no longer focused on impressing people of getting the latest gadgets. Moreover, you'll realize that a number of the items we consume are just status symbols. However, the truly rich don't have these items. That's because they prefer value over price. They want to get the best possible value at the lowest price.

When you sink into the investor mindset, you'll find that making the most of your investment capital then becomes your number one priority. You won't be looking to find new ways to spend your money. Rather, you'll be thinking about how to make your money grow.

Think about this scenario.

A new pair of shoes, which you don't really need, cost $100. This is money that will give you the momentary satisfaction of getting that new pair of shoes. Now, when you consider that $100 at 5% simple interest will become $105, you begin to see things in a whole new light. You begin to think, "why spend money on something I don't need when I can make it work for me?"

One of the most powerful realizations you can ever make is that money generated from investing is money you don't actually have to work for. When you receive interest, dividends, or profits, you are getting money that didn't cost you X amount of hours of hard work. Sure, you needed to work to raise the investment capital. But everything beyond that investment capital won't cost you hours of hard labor.

Do you see where we're going with this?

So, the savvy investor is always looking for ways to put their money to work for them. This is why the adage, "the rich don't work money" makes all the sense in the world. In fact, "money works for the rich." That's because they are able to put their money into a position where it generates income for them. Plain and simple. When you get this income, it will feel like free money. Of course, it isn't free, but you will get the feeling.

Setting the Right Objectives

When you set out in the world of investing, it's important to have the right objectives in mind. Unfortunately, many novice investors make the mistake of setting their sights too high. This is partly the fault of get-rich-quick schemes that you find everywhere.

An example of setting your aims too high could be quitting your job in a few weeks or transforming $500 into a revenue stream that generates thousands. Yes, it is technically possible to do so. For instance, FOREX allows investors to engage in high-frequency trading. This means that they can place a large number of trades in a short time period. As a result, the profits add up, thereby producing large gains. However, this isn't practical in reality.

This is why it's important for you to be sure about why you are getting into investing in the first place. For example, if you are drowning in debt and are desperate for money, you might take gambles when investing. As such, you may feel disappointed with the returns. Also, if you believe that you can achieve a lavish lifestyle within months of investing, then you might be surprised to find that building that kind of wealth actually takes years of careful planning.

This last point is not meant to discourage you.

It's meant to help you set your feet firmly on the ground. If you have the right expectations, you'll quickly learn that making a decent living from investing is quite straightforward. In addition, the simpler your lifestyle, the sooner you can stop depending on your paycheck.

Think about that for a moment.

There are lots of folks who make enough passive income from investing that they don't actually need to work. So, they end up working in something that truly makes them happy. While earning a paycheck is always good, they end up working in something that makes them feel fulfilled. In other cases, you find folks which such a basic lifestyle that they don't need more than a few hundred dollars a month to finance their basic needs. This enables them to volunteer and spend their time doing other meaningful things.

So, the first step to setting your objectives is determining the kind of lifestyle you want. Please bear in mind that the more lavish the lifestyle you want, the longer it's going to take you to get there. Now, make an approximate calculation of how much money you would need to finance that lifestyle. Don't worry about itemizing things to the cent at this point. The important thing is to have a ballpark. Then, go about determining how much money you need to make that lifestyle happen without having to depend on your paycheck.

Consider this example:

After crunching some numbers, you have determined that you need $3,000 a month to cover your living expenses. That works out to roughly $36,000 a year. To make this money from investing alone, we can assume a 5% annual return on your investment capital. To generate this much interest, you would need an investment capital of around $720,000. That might seem like a lot to you now, but the great thing about investing is that you don't need to work and save up this money. Your interest and capital will compound each other. This means that if you don't touch your earnings, both capital and interest will grow and grow.
What this example highlights is the fact that you don't need to be a millionaire to have a good life in which you don't have to depend on a paycheck. Over time, you will be able to free yourself from dependency on a single source of income. In fact, you can still keep your day job. The difference will be that your day job will not be your only source of income. It will be part of your overall revenue stream.

That's where real financial independence happens.

The most important step you can take right now is to forget about being a consumer and focus on being an investor. Whether you are investing in land, real estate, gold, oil, or stocks, you need to switch to a growth mindset in which money is just a vehicle for your ultimate goals. Money is just an enabler. You will also find that it's much easier to get to the point that you wish to be. So, don't despair. You will get there faster than you think. It's just a question of some hard work and careful planning.

Chapter 2: Learning the Rules of Investing

When you look at the world of investing, the stock market is just one of the types of investments you can make. The more you look into it, virtually anything can be an investment. Even your best friend's emu farm could be a good investment if it is set up correctly.

Now, we're not going to focus on your best friend's emu farm. We are going to discuss solid investments that you can make to help you get started on the road to financial freedom and independence. The spirit of this chapter is to figure out how these investments will help you get rich without having to bet the farm. You'll also find that it's quite easy to get started even with a few bucks.

One of the biggest misconceptions about investing is that "it takes money to make money." This mindset is permeated in the erroneous belief that you need to make a sizeable investment in order to make significant returns. While that is true in mathematical terms, it's not necessarily true in practical terms. You see, you don't need to have a huge investment capital to get started. As we have pointed out earlier, all you need is something to get started.

So, let's take a look at the various types of financial assets in which you can invest as part of your overall investment portfolio.

All About Financial Assets

There are a number of assets in which you can invest. Some are quite straightforward, while others are highly complex. We will look at all of them while trying to make things are easily digestible as possible.

Stocks

Stocks, or equities, are the most common financial asset you can trade. Stocks are nothing more than partial ownership of a publicly-traded company. The reason why companies are traded "publicly" is because anyone can buy into them.

Of course, you can't just go out there and buy stock. These companies' stock is traded on a stock exchange such as the one on Wall Street in New York City. To do this, you need to hire a stockbroker to conduct the actual trade on your behalf. This is why brokers take a cut from your winning. They need to make their salary and some profits for the company they represent. While there's nothing wrong with that, you need to be aware that not all brokers are created equal. So, knowing how much they charge will keep you from getting fleeced.

The essence of making money by trading stocks is to buy low and sell high. However, the reality is to buy as low as possible and sell as high as possible. This is where things get a bit tricky. Often, brokers and investors get caught up in their own greed. As a result, they tend to gamble far too much. When this happens, they take on too much risk. Therefore, they may end up engaging in risk trades that may lead them to lose significant amounts of money.

Another interesting aspect of stocks is that they produce dividends. "Dividends" are the share of the profit that shareholders receive at the end of the accounting year. Dividends are usually pennies on the share. But if you hold several thousand shares, you can make a good amount of money. This is why "blue chip" companies are sought after by investors. The term "blue chip" is used to refer to companies whose reputation and solid track record makes them stalwarts of their industry. These are companies that always turn and profit. Consequently, investors flock to these stocks as much as possible.

To trade in stocks, you can hire a broker to buy and sell shares for you. To do this, however, you need a significant amount of investment capital. This is where the "rich" investors club comes in. In these clubs, rich investors may pool their money together so that professional brokers can do the legwork for them. These clubs are often called "hedge funds." This is a fancy term to refer to groups of wealthy investors, which may include individuals and large corporations.

Retail investors, that is investors who don't have a large investment capital to work with, can buy a piece of the action through mutual funds, index funds, exchange traded funds (ETFs), and investment accounts such as a 401(k). These accounts pool the resources of retail investors and then divvy up the profits among all participants. These types of accounts generally offer market average returns. This implies that you can expect an interest rate of about 4% to 6% annually. You can then choose to roll over your investment after expiration or withdraw it. Most investors withdraw a portion of their earnings and roll over the rest.

Mutual funds are an investment vehicle in which retail investors are grouped together. These funds offer a diversified range of stocks. This means that these funds don't invest in a single company or industry. The fund may have a collection of companies across various industries. The point of doing this is to reduce risk. In a manner of speaking, money managers look to avoid depending on the performance of a single company or industry.

Index funds are another investment instrument that is intended to capitalize on a diversified range of stocks. The difference between stocks and mutual funds is that an index fund is tied to one of the major stock indices, that is, the Dow Jones Industrial Average, the S&P 500, or the NASDAQ. Depending on your particular preference, you can buy into the index fund that best suits your criteria. Generally speaking, the

Dow Jones is the largest of the major indices as it hosts the 30 largest companies in the United States. Also, the S&P 500 provides exposure to the 500 largest corporations in the United States. These two indices don't focus on a specific sector. If anything, they focus on a wide range of corporations. Therefore, you can buy into a fund that suits your particular interests.

As for the NASDAQ, this index track technology companies specifically. So, if you are keen on investing in the tech sector, this would be your first choice. Of course, there are other types of index funds that track industrial companies, mining, gas, and oil, among many other specific sectors. The best way to choose the type of industry you would like to invest in is by seeing which sectors offer the best returns based on your expectations. For example, mining, oil, and gas tend to make solid profits in the winter months when demand for heating goes up. Likewise, oil companies tend to have increased revenues during the summer months as gasoline demand picks up.

These are the types of analyses that you need to make in order to determine where to put your money. You can do this quite easily by staying up to date on the information provided by major news outlets such as Bloomberg, MSNBC, CNN, Financial Times, or Market Watch. Of course, there are many other business news outlets. Nevertheless, it's always good to cross-reference what you read.

One other way you can invest is to purchase stock through what is known as "private equity." This type of investment generally implies purchasing stock directly from a company. Large corporations offer this option to the average investor though it is quite hard to get your foot in the door. So, many wealthy individuals invest in startups. What these investors do is buy a percentage of a startup company in exchange for funding. The founders of the company use that funding to expand their operations and thereby grow the business. If the business takes off, the holders of private equity can make a killing. Just think about the investors that got in early on Facebook and Google. Now, the chances of you buying into the early days of a company with the potential of Google of Facebook may be slim, but if you can buy into a company that gets bought out by a giant corporation, you could really clean up.

Commodities
There are investors who would rather not invest in stocks but rather would prefer to invest in commodities. In short, commodities are physical goods that you can actually have delivered to your place of choice. The most common commodities traded on financial markets include oil, gas, metal (industrial and precious), agricultural products, cattle, and manufacturing. These goods are bought and sold on financial markets through investment instruments are known as futures, spot, and exchange traded funds (ETFs).

When you hear the term "spot," it means that you are buying contracts that are good for the delivery of the underlying asset at current market prices. This is important to note as current market prices are affected by the conditions of the market. So, if there is news of a potential oil shortage, investors will scramble to get their hands on any available oil contracts. This drives up the price. So, holders of contracts can make a killing.

To avoid getting pummeled in the open market, investors use "futures" contracts to lock in price. What a futures contract does is negotiate future delivery of the good at today's prices. The producer wins because they guarantee the sale of their production while investors ensure that they won't get rocked by sudden shifts in market prices. These contracts can be bought or sold depending on the expectations of the investor.

ETFs are instruments in which investors pool their money. These funds are then invested specifically into a given commodity. So, if you are interested in gaining exposure to the oil market, you can buy into an oil ETF. What the ETF does is provide returns based on the performance of oil. So, if oil goes up in price and investors make money, you win. If oil tanks, then your investment would lose money. That's the inherent risk of ETFs.

It should be noted that ETFs are a preferred vehicle by investors as they are able to buy into commodities which they feel have a good upside without actually having to deal with the commodity itself. After all, most investors aren't actually keen on having barrels of oil delivered to their homes.

Gold and other precious metals
You may hear about investing in gold and other precious metals (silver, platinum, and palladium) from time to time. Gold is an asset that is traded as a commodity though it has investment appeal. The reason for this is that investors traditionally take money out of the stock market and sink it into precious metals while the upheaval dies down in the stock market. You too, can gain exposure to gold in one of two ways; you can either buy physical gold or get "paper" gold. Paper gold is a term that is used to refer to gold-based ETFs. This is the preferred choice for most investors as they wish to gain exposure to precious metals without running the risk of having gold bars delivered to their door.

If you feel that gold is too expensive, you can always buy into silver. Silver is a much cheaper option. Platinum and Palladium generally trade for half the price of gold. So, if you are keen on gaining exposure to precious metals, you may consider buying into an ETF.

FOREX
There is an abundance of information regarding the FOREX market. This market is the most liquid market on the planet as you are dealing specifically with currencies. This means you take US Dollars and

convert them into Euros. Of course, you could do this for any currency on the planet. This market offers two ways of investing. One if a FOREX ETF in which you invest your money and allow money managers to handle the dirty work for you. The other is for you to trade FOREX directly. Tools such as MetaTrader 4 enable you to get your hands dirty in the FOREX market. Much like day trading (this is where you trade stocks yourself), you can cut out the middleman so you can make investment decisions yourself.

Investing in FOREX does require you to become familiar with the dynamics of the market. However, if you are interested in doing this yourself, you will find that FOREX is a great way to invest in your free time as it is a 24-hour market. This means you could trade at night or on the weekends. Plus, you can save a great deal of money in terms of fees and commissions. It is certainly a great option for anyone who wants to get hands-on experience.

Cryptocurrency
Investing in cryptos should be seen as a contact sport. Cryptos are not for the faint of heart as this type of investment does not have the kind of stability like stocks or commodities do. For instance, those who invested in Bitcoin went on a rollercoaster ride. First, Bitcoin traded for as little as $2 a coin when it first started. Then is exploded to a high of $20,000 a coin before crashing down to about $5,000. Since then, it has rebounded to about $10,000. That's an insane ride. Along the way, some investors cleaned up and

became millionaires. Others got completely wiped out. This is why cryptos are not for the faint of heart.

Still, you can gain exposure into this market either by investing in cryptos directly, that is, purchasing them yourself and then reselling them (much like you would gold) or by investing in a crypto ETF. Crypto-based ETFs are a rather new investment instrument. So, you should do your homework on them before buying into one. However, there are solid ETFs that offer exposure to a wide range of coins such as Bitcoin, Ethereum, Litecoin, among many others. The great thing about ETFs is that if you don't have $10,000 to purchase a single Bitcoin, you can buy partial ownership of one. As the valuation of Bitcoin increases, you make money. If the valuation falls, then your stake is worth less. Still, it's worth looking into as cryptos appear to be the wave of the future. Who knows if you buy into a cheap coin which could skyrocket in the same way that Bitcoin did?

Bonds
Bonds are another popular investment instrument. Bonds are debt that is issued by governments or corporations. These are then negotiated among investors as governments and corporations use them as a means of raising capital.

Firstly, there are sovereign bonds. These are issued by governments and can either be traded on a stock exchange or can be purchased directly through auction. For instance, the US Treasury issues bonds directly to a group of investors who are invited to the bond auction. The largest buyer of these bonds is the Federal Reserve (FED). The FED then issues Dollars into circulation. These Dollars are backed by the bonds the Treasury issued. As such, a regular dollar-bill is backed by debt, that is, the debt created by the US Treasury.

In the case of corporate bonds, these are backed by the corporation itself. So, if the corporation were unable to cover these bonds at some point, their insolvency would be covered by the sale of assets or the entire liquidation of the company. The proceeds would then be used to cover outstanding bonds, among other debts.

It should be noted that sovereign bonds are less risky than corporate bonds. However, some nations don't have the stability of others. This makes their bonds riskier as the likelihood of their default is greater.

You can invest in bonds, especially if you are looking for long-term investments. You can either purchase them from your broker, or through public auctions. In the past, bonds were used as a means of preserving wealth from generation to generation. However, be wary of inflation as a $100 bond was worth more 30 years ago that it is today. Nevertheless, if you have money that you don't plan to use in the short-term, you could get good returns on a bond.

Passive and Active Investing Through ETFs

Thus far, we have spoken a great deal about ETFs. The reason why ETFs have become so popular is that they give investors the opportunity to place their money exactly where they want them. This is why mutual funds don't offer any kind of control to investors. Investors simply entrust their money to a fund manager, and that's the end of that. As we have stated, this is not a bad thing. However, if you are more hands-on, the ETFs offer you a better opportunity to do so.

So, in this section, we are going to look at how you can be both an active and passive investor through ETFs.

Passive investing

ETFs are great for passive investors. They offer higher returns than the average mutual fund or investment account. When you buy into an ETF, all you are doing is putting your money into an industry, stock, or commodity that you feel has the potential to make significant returns. Since there is greater risk involved, ETFs tend to pay out more. Nevertheless, you can be relatively sure that you will get positive returns.

Now, depending on the nature of the ETF, you won't have to lift a finger. All you get is a statement at the end of every month telling you how your account is going. That's pretty passive. You may get a call every once in a while, from your broker asking you to top up your account or perhaps roll over your contract. In some cases, your broker may try to upsell you to a better performing ETF. Ultimately, that's your decision.

ETFs can provide you with good short-term returns, especially if the fund performs well. While they won't make you rich overnight, you can expect consistent returns, particularly in industries and goods which have a consistent track record.

Active investing
Now, if you are more hands-on, then you can purchase ETFs yourself as part of day trading. Also, you can work directly with a broker in managing your account. This is generally reserved for wealthier individuals who meet the criteria needed to have an account manager work with them one-on-one. If you meet these criteria, you can call up your broker and ask them to liquidate your position and move you into something else. After all, this is what you are paying for.

Likewise, if you qualify for a rich investors club, you can pull your money out at any time. Unless the contract binds you to a specific timeframe, you can ask your money manager to send you a check for your capital plus returns. In this type of arrangement, you hire the account manager to do the dirty work for you while you supervise the return on your investment while making decisions on the nature of the investments made on your behalf. If you like to get into the thick of things, this would be a great option for you.

Golden Rules of Money Management

All successful investors strive to create a discipline that can guide their investment decisions; this discipline is predicated on the fact that you need to have a clear investment philosophy. This is why having a loosey-goosey approach generally leads to underperforming results at best.

Additionally, being a successful investor is about having the right mindset. This is why we are going to look at three golden rules of money management, which you can use to help you guide your investment philosophy while ensuring that you make the best possible returns.

1. **Don't invest more than you can afford to lose**

This rule is about as ironclad as they get. Often you hear investors take out a mortgage on their home to invest in the stock market. Then, when the market tanks, they lose a significant chunk of their investment in addition to owing on the property. Needless to say, this is not a wise choice.

So, when you set about to invest, think about how much money you could reasonably afford to lose without it crippling your finances. If that's only $500, then that's what it is. Never bet your family's livelihood on investing. Since risk is an inherent part of investing, there is no telling what can happen at any given time.

2. Always have a plan

Even if you plan to be a passive investor, you always need to have a plan. Your broker can help you map out the kinds of returns you can expect to make based on the type of investments you have made. If you are more hands-on, then you can sit down and project how much money you can reasonably expect to make. Then, take that into account as far as rolling over your entire proceeds or perhaps taking a chunk out of your profits for other purposes such as paying down debt. In the end, having a plan is always going to work out in your favor, especially when things get rough.

3. Give your money a chance to grow

All investors look forward to seeing significant returns right away. However, your returns may not be astronomical right away. This is why you need to give your money a chance to grow. As your investment capital grows and grows, you will find that it will gain momentum. Eventually, you'll be able to make significant returns. That is why patience is a virtue that all investors need to have. If you are not willing to put in the time it takes for your money to grow, then perhaps you might consider more aggressive types of investing, such as starting a business.

With these golden rules, you'll be set for life. In fact, you'll find that making money through investing is quite straightforward when you know what to do and where you are going.

Mistakes to Avoid as a New Investor

The flipside of the golden rules is the mistakes that novice investors make. So, let's take a look at the top five no-nos that new investors make.

1. Not diversifying

This is essentially putting all of your eggs into one basket. When you don't diversify, what ends up happening is that you place your hopes on a single stock, industry, or asset class. In the worst of cases, you end up getting wiped out. In the best of cases, you end up with underwhelming returns.

So, the antidote to this mistake is to explore the various instruments. Successful investors have a combination of mutual funds, ETFs, commodities, and even private equity. This can help you offset losses while ensuring various revenue streams.

2. Taking on too much risk

While risk is an inherent part of investing, too much of it can put you in a bad place. Perhaps the biggest risk you can make is to invest in something you don't understand. For instance, if you are asked to invest in a business that you are not clear on how it will make money, you are taking on too much risk. This is why investors back away when they can't see how an investment stands to make money. This is something that you need to keep in mind at all times.

3. Spreading investment capital too thin

Since diversification is the antidote to risk, novice investors look to invest in everything they can. However, not all investments are good for everyone. You need to figure out which investments are good for you. Most importantly, you need to be cognizant of what each type of investment involves before jumping. So, it's best to start off with one type of investment before moving on to the next. It's always a good idea to master one before moving on.

4. Getting talked into investing

Salespeople are trained to get customers on board without actually going into the nitty-gritty of investing. If you are being hounded by a pushy broker or sales exec, it's best to slam the brakes. Any time you are getting pressured to invest in something, you are most likely falling into the trap of a desperate salesperson. Always invest in instruments you understand while also getting as much information as you can. To be proactive in this manner, you can conduct your own research. That way, the next time you get a call, you know where they are coming from.

5. The fear of missing out (FOMO)

This is a real psychological phenomenon. The clearest example of this is Bitcoin. When Bitcoin skyrocketed, investors felt the FOMO. So, they piled on, hoping to ride the wave. Some made money; some got crushed. If you see that everyone is rushing toward an investment, you're already too late. So, let the hype die down. Once the dust settles, you can waltz in and scoop up some real bargains.

Chapter 3: Low-Cost Investments to Make Your Portfolio Grow

Once you make the decision to get started with investing, it's important to note that investment does not come without a price. Thus far, we have talked about how much brokers make commissions on your investments. And while that is fair as far as it pertains to the service they provide, that money comes from your profits. This is what makes the process unfair. Stockbrokers and investment firms all make their money off their customers. The worst part is that most investors just look at it as part of the cost of doing business. But when you dig deeper, you find that they make a lot more than you think.

So, this chapter is all about determining the hidden costs that come with spending and how you should take these into account so that you are not paying a penny more than you should. Often, these means taking matters into your own hands. For instance, some investors choose to day trade or dabble in FOREX. That way, the fees they pay are less than those charged by brokers.

Of course, we are going to explore both sides of the argument so that you can make an informed decision when it comes to investing. At the end of the day, you need to do what's best for your portfolio and the wellbeing of your family. Ultimately, this is the reason why you are looking to invest in the first place.

The first thing to consider is if investing is something that you wish to pursue actively. To illustrate this point, consider this situation.

You are a respected professional in your field. For instance, you are a doctor, lawyer, engineer, and so on. As a result, you are paid well for your services. This means that the more you work, the more money you make. Any time you take off work is money you don't earn. In this situation, you need to determine how much a day, or an hour, of your time is worth. Based on that premise, would it make sense for you to take time off your regular occupation to day trade?

Chances are you would lose money.

Take a high-level attorney, the kind that charges $400 an hour. Unless this attorney can make $400 or more day trading, chances are they are better off hiring a money manager to oversee their investments. If they really want to be active, they can schedule a weekly call with their fund manager. That way, they can keep tabs on what's going on.

Now consider the flipside. You have some time on your hands. As such, you have decided to take up investing as a means of furthering your knowledge and put some money in your pocket at the same time. You might not be making $400 an hour, but you have a good job and make decent money. So, day trading is appealing to you as it is something you can do around your schedule. Plus, you can automate your trading so that you don't have to be physically at your computer all the time.

Here is a third scenario.

You look at day trading, FOREX, or even cryptos as something challenging that you want to learn as much as you can about. You don't really view it as a job or do it because you are desperate for money. You look at it as a learning experience. Consequently, the experience of managing your own investments and making money is something that appeals to you. So, you are willing to take on the challenge it represents.

All of these cases highlight various reasons for being more or less involved in investing. Yet, they are all examples of how you can still become an investor without having to give up your life to do so. Regardless of whether you are a high-priced lawyer or just an average citizen, you can make investing. All you need to know is the tricks of the trade. Furthermore, it's important to understand the underlying fundamentals of investing.

The Cost Associated With Investments

Part of understanding the fundamentals of investing is related to the cost that comes with investing. Unless you are a venture capitalist and directly finance upstart companies, you will have a cost associated with your investments.

So, let's break down each of the costs one by one.

Membership Fees

Depending on the fund you are looking to join, you may have to pay a membership fee. These fees are usually charged annually and serve to keep the lights on. This is where financial institutions and brokers cover most of their overhead. As a result, they need to charge customers some sort of fee for joining the club. The nature of the fund will tell you how much you have to pay. The wealthiest of investors will most likely pay a few thousand dollars a year to be a part of the club. However, this fee also ensures that only those who truly qualify can join. It's just a way of selling exclusivity.

When you join a fund through your local bank or investment firm, you don't typically pay any membership fees. And even if you did, they wouldn't be more than a few dollars a year. So, that's all well and good. However, that's a cost you need to factor in. Thus, it's a question that you need to ask your broker.

If you choose to go the day trading route, you'll also need to pay an annual membership fee for the use of the trading platform of your choice. In some cases, discount brokers don't charge a fee. They just make that money up elsewhere. Nevertheless, you would still have to pay some kind of annual contribution to keep the platform running.

Commissions

Commissions are the way in which brokers make most of their money. In fact, you'll find that most stockbrokers don't even make minimum wage; their entire salary is based on commissions. So, if they don't sell, they don't get paid. It's that simple. This is why stockbrokers are pushy. They will try everything they can to upsell you all the time. Moreover, don't be surprised if you get calls out of the blue offering you wonderful incentives to switch over to another company.

How does that happen?

There are times when brokers switch companies and then take their clients with them. That's how they get your name and number.

Typically, brokers charge commissions ranging in the 3% to 6% range. It's kind of like the going rate for realtors. The reason for this is that they are legally bound to a certain range. Otherwise, they would gouge you completely.

So, on top of membership fees, you have to pay commissions to your account manager for you running your portfolio. These commissions can really add up over time. However, be wary of discount brokers. They can offer you a 3% rate, or even less, but you really need to do your homework on these guys as they may be running their firm out of a garage. In that case, who knows what they're up to. So, it's always best to pay a little more, but ensuring that you are not taking on needless risk.

Taxes

Oh, and the government needs to get its cut, too. In this regard, you need to be cognizant of your particular state's taxes in addition to federal taxes. Generally speaking, investors pay capital gains tax. This is the same scheme as when you sell a home.

When you open up a brokerage account, most brokers deduct taxes from your earnings. However, not all of them do. So, this is something you need to ask about. If your broker does not deduct taxes from your earnings, then you will need to include this in your tax return and pay any taxes you are liable for. As such, you might very well be on the hook for both income and capital gains tax. Under some schemes, you might be able to deduct your capital gains tax from your income tax. This is useful, but you need to file for it. Nevertheless, it's an option you can consider.

On the whole, you can expect to pay a tax rate of about 15% to 20% on short-term gains, that is, gains made in a period of more than a year. For assets held less than a year, you may get slapped with taxes ranging from 10% to 37%, depending on your income bracket. So, if commissions and fees don't zap your winnings, taxes will.

However, there is some good news. If your income bracket is less than $40,000 a year, you might get away without pay capital gains, especially if your yearly earnings don't exceed your bracket. So, if you make a profit of $50,000, then you'll be in trouble. If your bracket is somewhere between $40,000 to $430,000, you can expect to pay about 15%. If you go over $430,000, then you'll likely be taxed at 20%.

To offset paying a hefty bill, some investors choose to hold on to their assets as long as they can. This enables you to reduce your bill or cut out taxes completely. For instance, mutual funds are not liable for taxation at maturity, depending on the scheme you are under. In the case of 401(k)s, you don't have to pay a penny in taxes if you withdraw it until you hit retirement age. These are two things to consider.

Also, check with your broker to see if they offer tax-exempt accounts. There are retail accounts that are aimed at very small investors. As such, these accounts are tax-exempt up to a certain threshold. So, it definitely makes sense to look into these. For instance, IRAs and Roth IRAs are accounts that you can take advantage of. They function similarly to 401(k)s but may offer much more flexible terms such as shorter investment periods or a limited amount of funds you withdraw annually without having to pay any kind of penalty.

How to Make Money From Various Investments

One of the keys to financial freedom is generating multiple revenue streams. Anything that puts money in your pocket is a revenue stream. Some produce a lot of cash, others not so much. However, when you add them all up, they really count.

The reasoning behind building multiple revenue streams lies in the fact that the more ways you have to generate income, the easier it will be for you to get away from depending on a single source. When you depend on a single source of income, such as your job, your finances are devasted when you lose it. However, when you build up multiple revenue streams, then you have the opportunity to make yourself less vulnerable to the ups and downs of the economy. Additionally, the loss of one revenue stream, such as your job, will not derail your finances. Sure, it might put a dent in your financial wellbeing, but it won't cripple your livelihood.

Successful investors are great at building multiple revenue streams. Some are active, and some are passive. Nevertheless, they are all contributing to building up a secure financial future. So, let's explore how you can make this work.

First of all, let's assume that you have a job. For a while, this is going to be your main source of income. This is going to be the source of income, which will lead to the creation of the other revenue streams that you will create. Consequently, you need to ensure that it remains steady for the foreseeable future. If you feel insecure about your future in your current job, then it might be a good idea to make plans in case you need to find another one.

Next, think about which of the investment instruments presented herein is best for you. For instance, if you have a busy schedule, you might not have a lot of time to devote to direct investing. So, a more passive instrument would work well for you.

Also, double-check with your employer if they make matching contributions to a retirement plan such as an IRA or 401(k). While we have outlined why these investments are not going to make you rich, they will help you generate income further down the road. So, it's the type of investment that you want to have just in case.

Then, take a walk to your local bank or call up your nearest broker. Interview regarding the various investment options they have for you. Perhaps a mutual fund or index fund may work out favorably for you. Some of these accounts can be opened with a little as $100 with monthly contributions. In some cases, these can be automatically deducted from your paycheck. So, it's definitely worth looking into.

If you are interested in getting your hands dirty, you can look into FOREX. You can either open up an account with a broker or venture out into your own trading platform. Please be advised that if you do decide to venture out into the world of FOREX trading, it is highly recommended that you study the market well.

In addition, please take a look at bonds. If you are looking for a safe, long-term investment, then bonds can be your best option. A lot of folks who receive an inheritance choose to buy government (not corporate) bonds. This is why in which you can ensure that an inheritance can be passed on from one generation to another. Plus, the biggest risk with bonds is the government going belly up. That's extremely unlikely. 15 to 30-year bonds are the safest. And don't worry if you need to cash them in early. You can always sell them. Of course, you might take a hit on them, especially depending on the market. Still, if you are in no hurry to spend the money you have today, bonds can provide you with a safe alternative.

Now, about real estate.

Commercial real estate is a dangerous game. When the market is rocking and rolling, occupancy is quite high. However, when the economy takes a downturn, it can derail your investment plans. If you seek to purchase rental properties, single-family homes are the hardest to rent out. So, apartments make the best options, especially if they are relatively affordable.

Here is the mistake that investors make when looking to invest in real estate. They look for bargains. You see, there is a reason why a property is cheap. Usually, it has to deal with the condition of the property itself. It could be that it needs a ton of work, or there is simply something wrong with it. In other cases, it's just located in a bad spot. The adage, "buy the best house in a bad block" is a bad idea when it comes to real estate. It's always best to buy "the worst house in a good block."

Ideally, you would have the money to purchase the property outright, thereby owing nothing on it. Now, if you were to finance it, then consider how much you would be able to put down and then what the monthly payment would be on the mortgage. Based on that, you can then calculate if the investment is worth it or not.

How so?

It depends on what the market rate for the rent would be. If you find that the rent is well below the mortgage payment, then you wouldn't be making too much off it. Ideally, the rent would be enough to cover the mortgage. So, even if you didn't make anything above the mortgage, you would at least have your tenants paying for the property.

Please bear in mind that investing in real estate can be a gamble, especially if you aren't careful about the place where you are buying. So, do keep this in mind when looking at property.

Profiting From ETFs

Throughout this book, we have spoken about ETFs at great length; the reason for this is that ETFs have a cross-cutting appeal across many different industries and asset classes. This makes it easy for you to have an array of choices from which you can find an investment that suits your needs.

If you are looking to play it safe, that is, not take on too much risk, then investing in a stock ETF would make sense for you. You can choose these products for a specific industry. For instance, you are knowledgeable about the mining industry. So, you can talk to your broker about the nature of the ETF and the companies they are planning to invest in.

Also, if you are familiar with commodities such as oil or precious metals, you can talk to your broker about their investment plan. That way, you can get a good idea of what they plan to do and how they plan on investing your funds.

In addition, it's crucial to understand what the dividend rate is, the commission, and any other hidden costs. For instance, some ETFs may ask you to invest a minimum amount of money. Otherwise, you may have to pay a maintenance fee for the low balance. In other cases, you may have to deposit the minimum amount required in order to stay in the fund.

As you can see, there are various types of conditions that you may have to meet to profit from the fund. Also, it's important to study the average return rate of the fund you are looking to invest in. That way, you can ascertain how much you can realistically expect. While no fund will guarantee you a specific return, it certainly helps to have a ballpark figure you can count on.

Please bear in mind that there are no guarantees. However, there is a great deal of upside to ETFs if you are wise enough to choose the right asset class. This is why we are going to take a deeper look at how you can make money from ETFs.

How ETFs Make Money

Let's explore the way in which the ETF itself makes money.

Regardless of the underlying asset that the fund trades in, ETFs make money by the price of the asset going up. They lose money if the price goes down. It's really that simple. So, brokers need to do everything they can to ensure that they don't get wiped out if there is a sudden fall in prices.

Generally speaking, significant fluctuations don't happen unless there is an unexpected event that sets off a sudden drop in prices. When this occurs, brokers need to do everything they can to liquidate their position before it's too late.

Let's take a classic example so we can highlight the dynamic of ETFs.

You decide that you want to gain exposure to the oil market. So, you buy into an oil-based ETF. In this fund, the fund manager or broker will go out and invest in oil. This could be through the purchase of oil futures or direct purchase contracts on the spot market.
Now, let's assume that the price of oil spikes due to increased demand for the summer season. The broker then sells a bunch of contracts they were holding for a solid profit. All of a sudden, they recoup their investment and a good profit on top. From there, the fund takes the profit and spreads it around among the investors.

Here's the catch though:

If you are unaware of what oil prices are like or what the market is doing, you'll take your broker at face value when they tell you that you made X amount of money. However, if you are fully cognizant of market performance, you can call up your broker and ask them about the performance of the fund. From there, you can determine if they are short-changing you. While you might not be able to get any kind of insight into the overall performance of the fund, you can at least see if that particular ETF is worth holding on to.

Now, let's assume the price of oil tanks due to increased supply and a drop in demand. This means that the contracts the broker is holding area actually worth less than their paper value. So, the broker really has no choice but to get rid of them. This is especially bad if they are nearing maturity. This forces the broker's hand. They must sell at whatever price point they can get. This means that the fund loses money. As a result, you lose money.

If you are on top of the situation, you can call up your broker and ask them about the situation. They will tell you everything is alright, but at least your broker knows that you are on top of the situation. At this point, depending on the nature of the fund, you can ask for your money back. If you are locked into that fund for a specific period of time, you have no choice but to go along for the ride.

On the whole, ETFs make money. Their returns are generally above the average return of the stock market. This is why ETFs are a great way of getting started in the world of investing.

Tips and Strategies for Investing in ETFs

Let's take a look at three bulletproof strategies that you can use to help you make money when investing in ETFs.

1. **Understand the nature of the ETF**. All too often, investors get talked into investing without fully understanding the nature of the investment vehicle. While this isn't inherently bad, it does make it tough to be sure about what to expect. This is why you need to ask lots of questions before committing. If the broker or sales rep you're speaking is not prepared to answer your questions, then they are not worth dealing with. If you already have a relationship with them, then they should be able to take the time to clear up any doubts you may have. In particular, focus on the term of the contract, any and all payments, dividend payout, and any taxed withheld. These are all important elements to consider prior to signing up. If you are unconvinced by any of these elements, don't sign up!

2. **Look at the underlying asset**. Whether the underlying asset is a commodity, stocks, or whatever it may be (cryptos, for instance), you need to understand how the fund stands to make money. If you can't seem to find a way in which the fund stands to make money, then you are being set up for a trip to the cleaners. This plays back into the old axiom of investing only in those businesses that you understand. So, if the structure of the fund seems convoluted, it's best to steer clear. For instance, back in 2007-2008, investors were pitched into mortgage-backed ETFs. These funds stood to

make money off the debt given to the homeowner. And look at how that turned out. So, it's important to do your homework before signing up.

3. **Run in the opposite direction of fads.** If you hear about a fund that everyone is getting into, stay away from it. The best funds are those which don't advertise. Why? Well, good products sell themselves. So, if you find that everyone is talking about investing in this or that, you need to take a close look at whether this investment is really all that it's cracked up to be. Think about Bitcoin. By the time the general public got into the craze of Bitcoin, early investors had already cleaned up. The last folks to get in were the ones who got stuck with the check at the end of the party. You need to avoid being the one who gets stuck with the check at all times.

On the whole, having a skeptical mind about most investments will save you a ton of headaches down the road. You'll be able to spot potential danger well before it hits you.

Chapter 4: Investing in Cryptocurrencies

It seems that cryptocurrencies are all the craze nowadays. Ever since Bitcoin skyrocketed to $20,000 a coin back in 2017, the average investor quickly caught on to the potential upside of cryptos. However, Bitcoin is a cautionary tale for all investors. Someday, business schools will use Bitcoin as a means of teaching their students the dangers of getting caught up in the hype of sensational investments.

When Bitcoin was first launched back in 2009, no one quite understood what it was all about. As a result, no one really paid attention to it. In the early days of Bitcoin, it sold for about $2 a coin. In fact, the creators of Bitcoin even gifted some of them to friends and associates as a token of their appreciation for this support.

Over time, investors recognized the potential of Bitcoin as a game-changer in the world economy. Indeed, Bitcoin did have the potential to be that game-changer that would usher in the age of the fully digital economy.

This created a hype surrounding Bitcoin that elevated its valuation. From $2 a coin, it steadily climbed to about $1,000 before taking off for the moon. It eventually reached $20,000 in late 2017. From there, the price plunged all the way back down to about

$5,000. Over time, the valuation has hovered around $5,000 to $10,000.

Now, the reason why Bitcoin is a cautionary tale lies in the fact that investors piled on as they saw the hype. It seemed that everyone wanted a piece of the action. Their hope was to get in at any price point and hope to sell when the price got higher and higher. However, investors quickly learned that this was not to be the case. In any hype, there comes a point in which investors run out. There is a point in which buyers eventually run out. This can happen either because the price is too high, or investors simply can't afford it. At that point, holders begin to sell only to find that there are no takes. Quickly, holders begin to get desperate and sell at any price. The price suddenly begins to plunge. In their desperation, holders are willing to take any price. There are some investors who believe they are picking up a bargain. Yet, they are only scooping up a depreciating asset. By the time the dust settles, a great deal of investors end up wiped out.

This example highlights how "bubbles" are formed. A bubble is when an asset's valuation is artificially inflated; that is, its price does not reflect its true, inherent value. In fact, the price valuation is the result of investors' perception of its true value. When the bubble eventually bursts, a group of investors is left with nothing but broken dreams.

Perhaps the worst part of the Bitcoin bubble was the fact that average citizens sold assets or took on debt to finance their investment in Bitcoin. Ultimately, they were left with a bad experience. This is why the Bitcoin bubble is something that you should keep in mind when analyzing a potential market opportunity.

Fundamentals of Cryptocurrencies

Cryptos are essentially a digital currency that is meant to replace the basic function of paper currency, that is, to facilitate trade and settlement of accounts. However, that is not all cryptos are intended to replace. Particularly, the core tenet of cryptos is its underlying technology known as the "blockchain."

The blockchain, also known as a "digital ledger," is meant to foster accountability and transparency. What this means is that users must verify transactions in such a manner that there is a third-party authentication of each transaction. This enables transparency in such a manner that all transactions are recorded and cannot be deleted.

The digital ledge is also intended to create a trust system which gives users the confidence in knowing that they are dealing with other users in a faithful manner. As a result, there are no hidden cheats or frauds when it comes to the use of cryptocurrency.

The way in which the blockchain authenticates transactions is through the use of a math equation. The solution to this equation verifies the transaction in such a way that it is recorded, and payment is released to the receiver of the crypto coin.

At first, this system was swift and very easy to manage. This was due to the fact that questions were simple enough for computers to solve in a fraction of a second. However, there was one important limitation; each problem could only be used once.

Now, this shouldn't be an issue as there is an infinite number of math problems which could be used for authentication purposes. Nevertheless, problems would eventually get harder and harder to solve. This requires not only more time but also more computing power. Up to now, the blockchain which served as Bitcoin's underlying technology has essentially run its course. The blockchain would now require massive amounts of computing power and electricity, which essentially makes it unsustainable.

The emergence of other cryptos has tried to remedy the problems faced by Bitcoin. One of the biggest problems with Bitcoin is that the authentication of transactions generates new coins. This is called mining. Now, not every transaction generates a new coin, particularly when existing coins are used as payment. However, the creators of Bitcoin have hinted at capping off the total Bitcoin supply. There is no official number yet, but this is one of the reasons why Bitcoin's valuation remains high.

To avoid supply issues, other cryptos have led to what is known as an "initial coin offering" or ICO. An ICO is essentially a new blockchain releasing a number of coins into the market without the need for third-party authentication to ensure its creation. To remedy the third-party authentication issue, protocols have been put in place so that there is no need for increasingly difficult math problems.

For now, there are over 5,000 cryptocurrencies out there. Some are niche currencies, such as those used by gamers on specific gaming platforms. Beyond that specific platform, they are useless. Others have been implemented as a digital token that can vouch for certain transactions. A good example of this is the digital tokens that are generated every time you conduct an online e-banking transaction. Your bank sends a code to your phone in order to verify the transaction and authenticate it.

These types of solutions have been implemented as alternatives to having processes like those used by Bitcoin. In the end, the cryptocurrency technology is becoming more and more reliable. This is something that is very important to investors as the Bitcoin bubble has made everyone in the crypto space wary of a new bubble emerging.

How to Invest in Cryptos

Investing in cryptos can be an interesting exercise in both business and technology. One of the axioms that we have repeated several times throughout this book is to always invest in instruments you understand. So, if you are not highly proficient in cryptos, it's a great idea to learn as much as you can about them before investing. That's why this book is a great place to start.

On the whole, investing in cryptos is pretty much like any other type of instrument out there. However, you need to be keen on the reason why you are thinking about dabbling in cryptos. As such, you need to start off by figuring out why you want to invest in this type of asset in the first place.

Generally speaking, there are two main reasons for investing in cryptos: short-term or long-term gain.

If you are seeking short-term gains, then cryptos may not be your thing. You see, the crypto market isn't quite developed as the FOREX market is. In that case, FOREX is great at producing short-term gains.

What's the reason?

The sheer trading volume of FOREX is massive. It is the only market that functions 24 hours a day. As such, there is no shortage of action. Even the stock market shuts down every day and closes on the weekend. So, it's rather tough to trade for the purpose of short-term gain.

In that regard, "short-term" refers to holding positions for minutes at a time.

That's something you can't really do with cryptos, at least not yet. Generally speaking, investors in cryptos hold their positions for various days. This means that you shouldn't expect action to get hot and heavy unless there were sudden developments that would greatly influence the market. So, if it is short-term gains you seek, crypto may not be your best choice.

That's why cryptos are better for long-term investing. In this regard, we mean "long-term" in a period that spans over a month. In fact, most holders of cryptos tend to flip them in about 30 days. The reason for this is the lack of trading volume that you might find in other markets.

Additionally, since cryptos don't trade so widely, shifts in price action tend to come a bit slower than you might usually think. Thus, it's best to keep this in mind. But if you are willing to hold on to your positions for a while longer, then you could potentially make some decent returns.

The question now becomes "how to get started investing in cryptos?"

There are a couple of approaches.

One is to take matters into your own hands. Since cryptos don't have nearly as much regulation as other assets, you can buy and sell them as if you were selling a car. Although, the best comparison to buying and selling, cryptos is gold.

You can buy investment-grade gold bullion from any dealer. All you need to do is make sure that they are not ripping you off by selling you fake gold. Then, you can take physical delivery of the gold, or better yet, walk over to your dealer and pick it up yourself. Then, you can stash the gold at home. Other gold investors choose to pay third-party storage. This means they will hire a vault company to stash their gold rather than keep it at home. This is far safer, particularly if they hold a fair amount of gold.

This comparison works well for cryptos as you can purchase cryptos directly without having to go through brokers or investment firms. Then, you can stash them in your digital wallet. This is far more practical than having to hire a vault company. In a manner of speaking you are, it's just that it's not a physical vault.

When you go about buying cryptos directly from other holders, you can do this through a coin exchange such as Coinbase. In this exchange, you have a number of users who come together to buy and sell cryptos. The guarantee that you have in this exchange is that users are verified. So, you have the exchange's guarantee that you won't be running into any monkey business.

This is important to consider, particularly if you are thinking about purchasing cryptos directly from another individual. Unless you know who they are and clearly trust them, it's best to stay away from this kind of transaction.

Once you have purchased your first crypto position, you can then wait for the price to jump. Then, you can resell for a profit. It's really that straightforward. However, the catch is waiting for the price to climb enough so that you can make a profit. Therefore, you need to keep in mind that prices fluctuate. That's why it's up to you to do your homework on this. Exchanges like Coinbase track the price action of all the cryptos that are traded on their exchange. This is a great tool to have as you can see the trend in price action. This will help you decide if it's worth getting into or perhaps sitting out until a more favorable position emerges.

Then, there are crypto ETFs.

This is a rather new investment instrument as cryptos haven't been around for very long. In this sense, brokers don't have much experience trading cryptos. So, returns aren't quite as solid as you might expect from other, more traditional ETFs. Nevertheless, a crypto ETF could be a good option for you if you are looking to gain exposure to this market but are not keen on actually doing the trading yourself.

It should be noted that crypto ETFs are widely offered. So, you may have to shop around to find a broker who is able to trade in this area. There is a word of caution though: since the regulation isn't nearly as strict for cryptos, you don't have much guarantee other than the broker's reputation. This is why it's important to make sure that you are dealing with reputable individuals. That way, you can be certain you won't get swindled by some unknown crypto investor.

Rules for Investing in Cryptos

When investing in cryptos, it's always good to follow a set of guidelines that can help you get the most out of your investment while keeping you away from possible scams. So, here are five golden rules for crypto trading.

1. **Investment time in studying cryptos**

This is something we have stated over and over. You need to invest in instruments that you understand. If you don't understand how you can make money investing in cryptos, then it's best to stay out of the market until you feel ready.

The reasoning behind this assertion lies in the fact that if you don't understand an investment, then the likelihood of you making a mistake is higher. Consider this situation:

You are well aware of the fact that cryptocurrency refers to "digital money." However, you are not fully aware of the various kinds of cryptos and their valuations. So, an unscrupulous broker might sell you a crypto ETF leading you to believe that you are investing in Bitcoin, when in reality, you are investing in other coins.

In this case, you get hoodwinked because you believe you're taking a position in Bitcoin when you are really buying into other coins, whichever ones they may be. This is important as the returns will be quite different. For instance, the price of Bitcoin might remain relatively stable, thereby offering modest returns in comparison to other cryptos, which may have had better performance.

The opposite may also be true. An unscrupulous broker may tell you that you are investing in a less expensive coin, when in fact, they are investing in Bitcoin. They clean up, and you get "modest" returns. Please bear in mind that this isn't quite illegal. It's dishonest, but not really unlawful. As a result, understanding the coins, their valuation, and price movements will help you keep your broker honest.

2. Don't bet the farm

This point is true of any investment. However, recent experience has taught us that it's easy to get caught up in the hype surrounding new coins. In particular,

ICOs tend to get hyped up by their issuers. As you get caught in the hype, you might be talked into paying more for the coins than they are actually worth. For example, each coin is valued at $5 apiece. Yet, you're talked into paying twice as much based on the premise that once the coin hits the open market, investors will double your stake.

That has happened before, and investors have been burned. So, never bet the farm. If you want to invest in an ICO, do your homework on the coin and its underlying technology. Then, make a fair market valuation by comparing it to similar ICOs. From there, you can gain a fair assessment of what the coin would really be worth on the open market. If you feel that comparable coins provide enough insight, then you can go ahead and invest. But do bear in mind that ICOs, much like IPOs, can go flat once the asset hits the market. This is why betting the farm never makes sense.

3. **Avoid the hype**

Whenever you read about a new crypto being touted as the next big thing, be highly skeptical. Often, you don't know if tech magazines and publications have a stake in a new coin. In a manner of speaking, this would be dishonest unless the publication fully discloses their involvement, should they have any. So, whenever you hear or read about a new coin being hyped, do your homework. If you do a cursory internet search, you may find that the hype is justified, or it may just be that, hype.

Moreover, if you begin to hear about cryptos from your neighbors, barber, or mechanic, then you are already too late. This is exactly what happened with Bitcoin. When average folks were flocking to get a piece of the action, the ship had already sailed on the real gains.

Please note that the best coins are the ones you never hear of.

Why?

Well, because they haven't gained traction or popularity yet. This is often due to the fact that they are unproven in practice. So, creators don't tout their coin, or blockchain for that matter, until they are sure it works in real life. This is why they will be dirt cheap at first. Investors will recognize this opportunity and take a flyer on the hope it will explode. If the coin happens to fall flat, the loss wouldn't be too significant.

4. Start of small

For new investors, starting off small is always the way to go. Starting off small could mean sinking $100 into a bunch of coins that are relatively cheap. There are some coins that run for a little as pennies on the dollar. However, these might be too cheap and represent very little upside.

Then, there are coins that trade for a couple of dollars apiece. These could provide a good possibility of making a profit as they might make significant gains in dollar terms. Now, regardless of whether you buy dirt-cheap coins or not, it's best to stay away from the big-ticket items like Bitcoin, Litecoin, or Ethereum. Litecoin, for instance, can set you back about $200 per coin. This might be a little too much to take on in the early going. You can confidently invest at this level when you have more experience. The reason for this is based on your knowledge and experience in the market. When you are familiar with the way the market will play out, you can then confidently take on bigger bets.

5. Don't be afraid of partial ownership

In the world of crypto, Bitcoin is still king. However, not many investors have $5,000 they can sink into a single Bitcoin. So, you can look into ETFs or other crypto funds that offer you the possibility of buying into partial ownership of a Bitcoin. While you would never actually own the coin itself, at least you would gain exposure to the market. This means that if the price action moves up, you would stand to gain in relation to the stake you own in a coin.

Similar funds exist for high-price assets such as gold or real estate. You buy into the fund, which then gives you partial ownership. You could take sole ownership of the asset if you invested enough. But for most investors, they don't really care about owning the physical item. They just want exposure to the market, and by extension, the returns that come with it. So, do take the time to look into the conditions your broker may offer you in terms of partial crypto ownership.

Mistakes to Watch Out for When Investing in Cryptos

Being new to the investment world is never easy. There is always the possibility that you could make mistakes due to your lack of experience. Later on, you may regret the mistakes you made out of ignorance. That's why we are going to look at the five most common mistakes new investors make when they enter the crypto space.

1. Trading with other individuals

If you choose to purchase cryptos directly from other individuals without going through an exchange, then it's best you know who they are. There are a lot of crypto scams out there in which unscrupulous individuals purport to hold a "stash" of Bitcoin. There have been bogus auctions that are intended to lead on unsuspecting folks.

In this case, it's always best to have some sort of assurance that you are dealing with a real person. In fact, there are cases where hackers steal cryptos from other users, and they quickly pawn them off to would-be investors. Then, the real investors get caught with the coins and subsequently accused of perpetrating the hack or at least hiring the hackers to work for them. Needless to say, this is something that you want to avoid at all costs.

2. Purchasing unknown coins

These days, practically anyone can create a crypto coin. You can call it whatever you want and use it anywhere you wish. Most of the coins that you find are used for some specific purposes, such as in-game purchases on gaming platforms. That's all well and fine. However, things get dicey when you hear about some unknown coin that is being hyped (by unknown individuals) as the next big thing.

Here is where you have to do your homework.

If the new coin checks out, then you might consider investing a small sum of money on it. You should never sink more than a couple of dollars per coin on an unproven coin. If anything, you can get them for pennies per coin. Coins don't reach double-digit valuation until they have proven to be both practical in real life and sought-after by investors.

In the event that you choose to take a flyer on a new and unproven coin, please be aware that you may have to hold on to it for a while. If you expect to make quick gains, but may not get a lot out of it. Ultimately, you may end up holding a crypto that doesn't have very much of a future. However, you wouldn't lose much on it as you didn't pay a hefty price for it. This is why we always say that doing your homework is vitally important.

3. Buying gaming platform coins

As mentioned earlier, gaming platforms use their own coins for in-app purchases. This is nothing more than a marketing gimmick that's used to disguise the real cost of the items you are purchasing. While some platforms allow you to mine for coins, such as completing levels or issuing coins after a certain length of playing time, the truth is that buying the coins with the intent of re-selling them is a waste of time and money. No one is going to buy the coins from you if they can get them from the gaming platform directly. It would make sense if you could get them for free, say by breaking into someone else's account, and then selling them at the same price as the platform, or lower. Beyond that, it doesn't really make sense to try and resell coins from gaming platforms.

4. Looking to make an immediate profit

When it comes to cryptos, it's best to have a "wait and see" attitude. Those who are looking to make immediate profits would be better off in the FOREX market. This is a highly liquid market that could potentially land you profits in a matter of minutes.

At the moment, investing in cryptos is more about patience. If you have the time to wait a couple of weeks to see where price action may lead you, then you have a chance to make some good returns in cryptos. This "wait and see attitude" is the reason why you should not sink too much money into a single coin unless you know they are a proven commodity such as Bitcoin, Litecoin, or Ethereum.

5. Buying up as much as you can

With the number of coins on the market today, it's virtually impossible to try and corner a specific market. Moreover, buying up massive amounts of coins, even if they cost pennies on the dollar, doesn't really make much sense. This is especially true if the supply is in the millions. The reason why it's useless to try and buy up as much as you can lies in the simple law of supply and demand. It would make sense to try and corner a coin that has a limited supply. Unless that's the case, you would be better off taking positions in various coins. This is an example of diversification, and it can help you offset the possible losses from one coin with the gains from another.

Chapter 5: Making the Right Investment Decisions

Being a successful investor boils down to making the least number of mistakes. It's a given that all investors make mistakes. However, the most successful ones are the ones who avoid making disastrous mistakes.

Overall, making mistakes is a part of the learning process. However, there's a difference between taking your share of lumps while getting the hang of investing, and then there's making catastrophic mistakes that would cripple your portfolio.

Let's consider an example of this.

Investors generally get caught up in their emotions. After all, it's perfectly natural for humans to get wrapped up in their emotions. We wouldn't be human if we didn't. Nevertheless, it's important to keep emotions in check, particularly when you are going through a cold streak.

Some investors get caught up in their emotions when they are losing money on a deal. Often, investors choose to stay in far too long in the hopes of recouping their losses at some point. However, there comes a time when you simply need to cut your losses and get out.

This is a very important thing to keep in mind every time you invest. Unless you are planning on staying invested for the long haul, cut your losses as soon as they emerge. There is no telling how long it will take to recover your losses, if ever.

The difference between staying invested for the long haul and staying in too long lies in your objectives. For instance, if you purchase a 401(k), then you know you have to stay in until you retire, basically. But if you are looking to purchase an ETF which you can liquidate at any time, it's best to dump it as soon as the market starts to sour. There is no point in waiting for the market to rebound. It could take weeks, months, or even years for the market to come back to your starting point.

In the event of investing in private equity, that is, a startup company, for instance, it's best to pull out when you see trouble ahead. Now, it's one thing to go through growing pains, and it's another entirely different thing trying to ride out a company that's in trouble. If you choose to hang tough, you'll most likely sink right along with the company.

These examples underscore the need to rein in your emotions. You cannot let your emotions get the better of you. If you fail to do so, you'll only open the door to trouble. Once you get into trouble, your only choice will be to pull out for good. You can't expect for things to suddenly turn around. While it is entirely possible, the likelihood is quite low. In fact, it's much likelier that things will go south before they turn around.

With that in mind, let's focus on the right decisions you need to make when it comes to investing. When you make the right decisions most of the time, you'll find it a lot easier to sleep well at night.

Converting Dividends Into Income

A common misconception that novice investors hold true is "it takes money to make money." While it would certainly be nice to place a few million dollars into a high-yield investment account and call it a day, the fact is that you don't need massive amounts of capital to make money. All you need is to get started with whatever you can do.

For some, this could mean getting started with as little as $50. This is certainly better than nothing. Of course, it might seem like it would take you forever to reach your desired goals. But when you think about it, you don't need that long to make headway.

One of the secrets to making money over the long run is converting dividends into income.

A mistake that some investors make is to withdraw the entirety of their dividends at the end of each period. So, if they invest $100, they take their winnings and reinvest the same $100. While this is not a bad idea, the fact is that you will never grow your capital that way. In fact, you would need to make another sizeable contribution in order to increase your dividends.

So, what can you do?

The answer lies in the power of compounding. This is the famous strategy purported by Warren Buffet.

To make this work, you need to high-yield account that will pay interest as often as possible on the balance of your account. Some high-interest accounts capitalize on interest on a monthly basis. The high rollers may open up accounts that capitalize on interest on a daily basis. But for the sake of this book, let's assume you have monthly capitalizations.

When you have monthly capitalization on the balance of your account, you set yourself up for massive gains down the road. At first, your gains may seem insignificant, but as your balance grows, you'll start to see the fruits of your labor.

The secret here is not to withdraw your interest payments. In fact, what you need to do is simply roll over your initial contribution, plus the interest that it generates. If you are able to make additional contributions, then your dividends will grow even faster.

Let's consider this example.

You start off with a $100 contribution. This pays 1% monthly on your balance. After the first month, you $101. So, instead of withdrawing the $1 worth of interest, you roll it over. Now, the interest payment is calculated over $101. That would give you $102.10 after the second month. After the third month, you would have $103.02, and so on. For the sake of simplicity, we have used a minuscule amount. However, when you project that over a 5-year period, you would have $721 while including monthly contributions of $10. If you had just saved up the $10 a month plus the initial $100, you would have $700. This means that you basically have a 21% rate of return over a 5-year period.

No investment can trump that. The stock is not even close. In a good year, you would expect to make somewhere around 5% on your portfolio. However, it's not likely that the stock market will give you a consistent 5% return every year. Some years will be good, and some will be bad. But let's assume that you do get a consistent 5% return over a 5-year period. That would put you at a 25% return rate over those five years. But, you would not get the benefit of compounding interest over your lifetime.

This is why the power of compound interest can help you become both a saver and an investor in the long run. The great thing about it is that you don't have to start off with a huge sum of money. You can simply start off with what you have and roll it over.

Once you have reached a point in which your capital has rolled over significantly, this same amount of money would be able to pay for your expenses as you reach retirement. After all, everyone's biggest concern is what to do at the tail end of their lives when they can't work anymore. This is the reason why investments such as a high-interest account can help you find a good way of earning an income right when you're about to reach retirement.

At this point, your investment should be able to give you a fair sum of money, which could finance your retirement. In this regard, the simpler your lifestyle, the less money you are going to need when you stop working. This is an important consideration to make as the more extravagant your lifestyle becomes, the more money you are going to need to finance it.

Now, this doesn't mean that you need to become a miser and live off scraps. What it does mean is that you need to be careful about where your money goes. Ultimately, the sooner you start investing, the more money that you will have. This is what can enable you to have the kind of lifestyle you want.

In retirement, folks only withdraw the monthly interest that this type of account generates. What it does is it allows you to keep your principal (the main sum that's invested) while it continues to produce dividends month after month. When you think about it, this is the type of investment that you can essentially set up and forget about. Otherwise, there is always a temptation to dip into those savings whenever you want something. Sure, there are emergencies. But as long as you don't touch those savings, you'll be able to watch your nest egg grow.

Proper Asset Allocation Based on Age

In this section, we are going to discuss a classic rule of thumb that rings as true today as it ever has. This rule isn't so much an iron law, but it is a pretty good way of determining your asset allocation. It can help you to organize your portfolio in such a way that you are able to manage risk while also giving yourself a chance to be successful.

This particular rule deals with stocks. So, it's important to consider that you would not only be dealing with stocks, but also other types of investments. Therefore, you need to keep an open mind when it comes to your asset allocation.

For this setup, time is of the essence. This means that the younger you are, the greater the amount of risk you can take. Conversely, the older you are, the less risk you can afford to take. This is crucial to keep in mind as the older you are, or at least the closer you get to retirement, the less you can afford to be wiped out by a sudden shift in the market. Plus, you need to be very careful that you don't take on any more risk than is absolutely necessary.

In essence, this rule says that you should subtract your age from 100, whereby the result should be the proportion of your portfolio that should be invested in stocks.

For instance, if you are 20 years old, then you can allocate 80% of your assets in stocks (100 – 20 = 80, that is 80%). The reason for this assumption is that you would have roughly 40 years before you hit retirement (assuming that's 60). Under this premise, you can afford to stay invested in stocks as you have the time to ride out any downturns in the market. So, even if the market tanked today, you wouldn't really need your money until you hit 60 or 65. Theoretically, that should give you enough time to recoup your losses.

Based on this rule, your asset allocation should look something like this: if you are 30, then you should have 70% in stocks if you're 40, then 60%, and if you are 50, then it should be 50/50. At 60 years old, your allocation should be 40% stocks while at 70, you should have 30% in stocks. As you approach 100, your allocation in stocks will essentially reduce all the way to 0%. This reflects the sense of urgency that comes with being unable to wait for the market to turn should there be a sudden downturn.

On the whole, long-term investors in the stock market do reap the rewards of their patience. However, we are talking at least 20 years of patience. This means that if you are not quite so young anymore, it's important to look at other potential means of investing your money.

Now, there is one interesting thing about investing when the economy is in a recession. You see, it's a drag to be invested and have the economy enter a recession. You automatically lose a portion of your portfolio simply because the market takes a hit. Depending on the severity of the recession, you may come out relatively well. However, if there is a catastrophic market downturn, you might end up taking a bigger hit.

As a reference, those who were invested in the stock market back in 1929 eventually saw 90% of their portfolio evaporate. Those that had the luxury of patience saw the market recover approximately 25 years later. However, this is an extreme example as the market crash of 1929 was a once-in-a-lifetime event. The garden variety recession usually takes no more than a couple of years to shake off the cold streak and then gain momentum once again. The period following the 2008 financial crisis led to one of the longest periods of economic expansion in history.

So, the question begs, if you are not invested in stocks, then what should you invest in?

Again, the answer to that question depends on age.

The younger you are, the more you can afford to have your investments tied up for the long haul. So, younger investors can look at assets such as bonds and ETFs. These are great for investors in their 30s and 40s.

Older investors need to have their assets as liquid as possible. This means that they need to have their money as readily available as possible in case of emergencies. Particularly high-yield accounts that don't have a fixed term to them work well. Also, money market accounts are a great choice. These accounts are highly liquid and can be cashed in at any time. For instance, certificates of deposit (CD) are a great way of having cash earn some interest while it sits in the bank. In the specific case of CDs, these are available in any number of terms. Most investors opt for 30-day CDs and simply roll them over at the end of every month.

Of course, it's important to note that a slice of cash on hand is also important. So, having some money deposited into a regular checking account is always useful, especially considering that you might have a need for cash at any moment's notice.

As for your emergency fund, putting it into a CD is actually a pretty good idea. Since you are saving this money for a rainy day, it helps to keep it stashed in an interest-producing account. That way, your fund will actually grow rather than just sitting idly in a regular non-interest yielding checking account.

On the whole, time is ticking. So, the sooner you can start investing, the more time you will have to get ahead of the game. But that doesn't mean that older folks can't get ahead of the game. It just means that you have to save more in order to catch up. The good news is that older folks generally carry less debt and less expenses. This is especially true for older folks who have grown children who no longer depend on them. As for younger investors, having a young family and a mortgage to pay off can be holding you back. But that shouldn't stop you from squirreling money away into income-producing assets. Ultimately, you'll regret not having started sooner when you see how much money you stand to make.

Diversification as a Means of Balancing Risk in Your Portfolio

Risk is an inherent part of investing. This means that there is always a chance that something could go wrong. Even if you do everything perfectly, you will still find yourself with some kind of risk. This is why nothing is totally certain in investing.

The reason for risk is that all assets are subject to market forces. Unless the price of everything was regulated to the degree where the effects of supply and demand could be erased, there will always be risk. Generally speaking, whenever humans are interacting, you have market forces. Thus, you need to be keen on making sure that you have the right measures in place to protect yourself against risk.

There are many ways in which you can protect yourself against risk. One way is to study the markets as deeply as you can. When you do this, you are able to gain insight into everything that could possibly happen at any given point. When you fully understand the dynamics of a specific market, you're able to gain a much better understanding of what could go right and what could go wrong.

With this in mind, careful study and planning are always a winning formula. The worst thing that you could possibly do is become an investor without having any sort of knowledge regarding the type of investment you seek to make. Of course, if you are more interested in putting your money to work and forgetting about it, the safer risks such as mutual funds are the best choice.

Now, why do we say these investments are "safer"?

The reason for this is due to the fact that mutual funds (or index funds for that matter) are generally highly diversified. This means that they are not invested in a single company or a single industry. Money managers look to invest in all of the best companies. This means that if there are a million good companies, they will try to gain exposure to all of them.

What diversification across a range of stocks does is give you the chance to offset your losses. For instance, if company A's stock goes down, you can make that up with the rise in Company B's stock. However, if you were solely invested in Company A, you could potentially take a massive hit if the company sinks.

But diversification isn't just about a wide range of stocks. It's also about gaining exposure to other types of assets as well. So, if you want to have a more balanced portfolio, then consider investing in CDs, bonds, real estate, commodities, and ETFs. As you can see, this wide array of investments allows you to place various amounts of money in different asset classes. If one asset class were to go through the roof, then you make a good deal of money. In contrast, if one asset class tanks, then the hit isn't nearly as severe as if you were invested in a single asset class.

When you apply the right asset allocation, you can then take the rest of your investable assets and place them into other classes. For instance, if you are 35 years old, then they recommend allocation for stocks would be 65%. That leaves 35% for you to explore other asset classes. Let's say that you are interested in gaining exposure to oil. You can invest in an oil-based ETF. Perhaps you are also interested in FOREX. So, you can take 30% for oil and 5% for FOREX.

It is not recommended for you to invest more than 5% of your total portfolio on a new asset class. So, if you are investing in something like FOREX or crypto, that is investments that you aren't quite familiar with, allocating a total of 5% would keep your portfolio safe.

Please bear in mind that successful investors are always looking for the best way to improve the distribution of their portfolio. Please don't think that you need to shed one investment so that you can enter another.

On the contrary!

The more assets you can accumulate, the more revenue streams you can create.

Passive Income From Investing

Once you have acquired enough assets, the kind that produces income, you can then receive what is known as "passive" income. Passive income essentially means that you receive income from investments for which you didn't actively work. A good example of this is a CD. The interest you receive from a CD is passive because you didn't need to actively participate in the money management process. All you did was deposit your money in an account while the bank's money managers took care of the rest.

As such, you could generate all kinds of passive income from all of the asset classes that we have discussed. For a lot of folks, real estate is the ultimate form of passive income. They buy rental properties that produce a monthly income in the form of rent from tenants. It's a great way for individuals to make money without "working" for it.

Perhaps the best thing about passive income is that it enables you to continue working. This is important as the goal here is not to spend the rest of your life sipping cocktails. The idea here is for you to have enough flexibility so that you don't depend on your job. Now, it's important for you not to neglect your job as you might social security benefits to collect at some point, or you might actually like your job.

One other important thing about passive investment is that it allows you to add various revenue streams in addition to your job. This is especially true if you are working in a good-paying. For other folks, passive income enables them to quit their job and start a business. If you have the knack for business, then a good business idea will help you multiply your earnings even further.

Please bear in mind that the name of the game here is flexibility. The more income you are able to generate, the more flexibility you have. When you don't depend solely on one form of income, you will have the freedom to make a lot more choices. Consequently, you will be able to live the life that you want to live without being concerned about paying the bills.

Automating Investments

One of the biggest problems that folks have keeping track of their investments. This can be tough, especially if you have a job, a family, and other responsibilities in your community. As a result, paying attention to investments can be a bit tough. Of course, it's important, but when you are really busy, some things might slip through the cracks.

This is why automating your investments can be a great way of helping you stay on track.

One such example is enabling automatic deductions from your checking account into your investment account. You can do this for high-yield accounts, 401(ks)s or even mutual funds. When you automate your contributions, the bank will simply deduct "X" amount from your bank account at certain intervals, say, at the end of the month. That way, you don't need to think about making a deposit into the account. All you do is set it up once and let the money to its job.

Also, you can automate the rollover of CDs, ETFs, and other types of instruments that have an expiration date. However, do be careful as automating the rollover of these instruments may lead you to have trouble accessing those funds later on. So, be cognizant of how and when the instrument rolls over. That way, you know when you can access the money should you need to.

Lastly, automating your emergency fund is crucial. A lot of folks prefer to create a separate bank account and enable automatic deductions into that account. The reason for this is that it takes the temptation away from them. If you just see the money sitting in a bank account, it can be tempting to dip into every time you want something. Now, it's one thing to use that money when you need to. But it's an entirely different thing to touch it for non-emergency needs. So, creating a separate account helps to reduce the amount of temptation you have.

On the whole, automation is about giving your mind a break from the various tasks you need to deal with. If you want a more hands-on approach, then you can shut off the autopilot and fly solo. However, this would require more time and attention. Nevertheless, if you are keen on staying on top of your assets at all times, then you can definitely do so. Still, automating some investments that don't require a great deal of attention will help you get a better handle on those investments which do require greater attention.

Chapter 6: Knowledge Is Not Power... Action Is!

The phrase, "knowledge is power" is quite true. Those who know have the power. This means that you have the opportunity to convert your knowledge into a benefit for you and your family. However, knowledge only becomes power when you are able to put it into action. You see, knowledge is essentially meaningless unless you are able to translate it into action.

This is the key to making this phrase truly powerful.

When you are unable to convert knowledge into action, all you have is the understanding of a given discipline but nothing more. This means that if you know how to make money, money won't appear in your life unless you actually do something about it. Thus, action is just as important as knowledge. When you combine both, then you are really setting yourself up for success.

However, most folks are great at finding any number of excuses. They will find clever ways of justifying why they can't do one thing or another. This is important to keep in mind. Often, you find that most folks will complain that they can't save any money because they have so many expenses. Sure, it's true that life isn't cheap. It's also true that we have so many expenses on a monthly basis. Yet, many folks who claim that they don't have a chance to save make this claim without actually going through their finances. If they did, they would surely find one way or another to save money.

The point here is not to slash your monthly budget in half.

The point here is to find holes in your budget. When you find them, then you are able to detect leaks that you can plug up. When you plug up your leaks, you are then able to save some cash. Even if it's just $50 a month, that's better than being in the red every month.

Additionally, discipline is a vital element. When you are able to develop discipline in your life, you can chart a course and stick to it. This is why the most successful investors lead very structured lives. They do so because they know that if they didn't, they would lose far more than just time.

As you become more and more cognizant of the fact that time is money, then you begin to realize that time and money are related directly. Now, this doesn't mean that you should spend every waking moment working obsessively. What it means is that every minute you are not investing is a minute you are wasting. Sadly, time does not come back, no matter what we do. The time that has already passed will never return. This is why you cannot afford to let another minute go by without doing something.

Also, we discussed how most folks seek to invest for the purpose of financing their retirement. Yes, this is an important part of all our lives. To all of us, old age is something that we need to take quite seriously. Otherwise, we may not be ready for when the time eventually catches up to us.

In this regard, it is of the utmost importance that you take what you have learned in this book and translate it into action. Most importantly, take the time to make a concerted plan. When you make a serious plan, you will be able to see how the path is laid out in front of you. Consequently, you'll be able to plan for the rest of your life. In the end, the only thing you'll have to worry out is fine-tuning your trading strategy.

But that starts now, that starts today. If you don't act sooner, you may come to regret the time you are letting go by.

The First Steps You Can Take as a New Investor

Truthfully, being a new investor can be daunting. There are so many options to choose from. There are so many things you could do with your money. There are also so many mistakes which you could make. This last statement isn't mean to discourage. Rather, it's meant to help you focus on the reality of investing. You need to keep your eyes on the prize. Otherwise, it can be quite easy to make a mistake.

Starting out in the world of investing doesn't have to be hard. After all, a book such as this one is a great way to get started. This information is the kind that you need to keep close to you at all times. That way, you'll develop your own investing philosophy based on sound principles.

The great thing about being an investor nowadays is that there is so much information on how you can do things right. In the past, information wasn't so readily available. As such, the only way you could truly become a great investor was to make your share of mistakes. In a manner of speaking, you had to pay for your education as an investor.

Today, "paying" for your education as an investor is reduced to spending some money on books and courses. This is money well spent as it will enable you to generate more money. Any time that you are able to make an expense, which will then enable you to make more money, is a worthwhile expense.

To get started, the first and most important step is to make up your mind to do it. You need to make a decision within yourself. You need to consciously say to yourself that you will do it, get going, and then stick to it. Once you have truly made up your mind to become an investor, then the rest of the way falls into place.

The next step is to set clear expectations. When you set clear expectations, you know what you can reasonably expect and how long it would take you to get there. Now, there is nothing to say that you should wish for a simple lifestyle or that you should short-change yourself. If you wish to have a lavish lifestyle filled with exotic trips, that's fine. However, you need to be aware of the fact that financing such a lifestyle is not easy.

By setting realistic expectations, you can then focus your investment decisions on reaching those first goals. For instance, you have determined that it is realistic for you to save $100 a month. So, you make up your mind to save $100 every month. To make that happen, you open an investment account and automatically deduct those $100 from your account every month. Since you have automated your savings, you won't be able to do anything about it. Once the money hits your account, it's moved over into the investment account.

At first, it might not seem like you'll become rich any time soon, but just making a start is enough to get the ball rolling. Over time, you will not only have money saved up, but that can open up to bigger and better things.

After you set your expectations, you can then begin to study the types of investments that would seem most reasonable to you. You can begin by looking at the opportunities you have at work. If you have the chance to sign up for a 401(k) with matching employer contributions, then you should not think twice about it. Sure, the stock market is quite volatile, but at the end of the day, you are basically getting free through the matching contribution scheme. Plus, it's money that you will never be taxed on.

In addition to any investment schemes based on your job, you can also look into what investment accounts your local bank has to offer. You can look into mutual and index funds while also exploring the benefits you might get from a CD or high-yield investment account. It could be that you can find a good choice for you at this point in time. This is key, as you may not have a lot of money saved up. So, if you can get started even with $50, you can at least do something to help you get something back for your hard-earned money.

As you begin to gain momentum, you can then look into other types of investment. Perhaps you might be looking into ETFs or even putting some money aside to invest in government bonds. If you can spare some money that you are sure you won't need in the short-term, you can consider these types of investments. All the while, you are working your day job as if nothing was happening. Yet, you have your money working for you in the background.

Eventually, you'll have enough money to consider other larger opportunities. For instance, you might consider starting a business or investing in real estate. While there are much more ambitious goals, they are certainly worth looking into at some point. In fact, you'll be surprised that you get better opportunities simply based on your track record as an investor. Banks love it when their customers have good track records. The reason for this is that they know that you can be counted on to save money. If you also keep a relatively low debt level, you can qualify for additional loans and mortgages, which can help you purchase an investment property.

Do you see how investing, even if it's just a little, can snowball?

This is why we have repeated throughout this book that you need to get started even if it's just with a modest sum of money. In investing, there is no sum too small. While the returns may not be astronomical at first, over time, you'll get some good returns on your money. This is why you need to get started as soon as you can. That's how the expression "time is money" came into being.

How to Have Fun While Making Money

Even though investing is a serious business, there's no reason why it should have to be painful or unpleasant. The fact is that investing is something that you should enjoy simply because you are making money. Still, you can also enjoy investing because it's the type of activity that can lead to a great deal of learning.

You see, beyond making money through your investments, the action of investing is also a question of learning valuable life skills. Sadly, there are many opportunities out there for the average person to make money. However, we aren't generally taught about these skills in real life. In the best of cases, we learn these skills from our parents. But as for school, you don't learn about investing unless you go to business school. This means that it's not so easy to learn about the world of investing.

Additionally, we don't normally learn about managing money and handling finances. As a result, we go through life learning about money the hard way. This means that we need to first learn from our mistakes before we can confidently use our money to our own advantage.

So, when you seriously get into investing, you learn about so much more than the way financial instruments work. You learn about managing money and about how to get a handle on your emotions. This is why making money should be something enjoyable. Even if you don't like financial matters, or if they seem boring to you, at the very least, you should feel comfortable with the idea of learning about how you can make money while going about your usual life. This, in itself, is one of the best ways in which you can make your life that much better.

Perhaps the most enjoyable part of the entire process is figuring out what kind of life you are building. Sure, the entire planning process, particularly managing a budget, can be time-consuming and somewhat tedious. Still, it's important to take the time to plan out what you want to make of your life. This is where you can use your creativity and let your imagination soar. In the end, this is what makes life that much easier to deal with.

This is why we would like to encourage you to make the most of your imagination to plan the life that you have always wanted to lead. Building your future life (along with your family's) ought to be a process that motivates you to keep going. Otherwise, it wouldn't make any sense to do it. Of course, we all need to exercise patience throughout the entire process. But the satisfaction that comes with knowing that you were able to build your life exactly the way you planned it does not have a price.

Seeking Other More Experienced Investors

Another important characteristic of successful investors is that they had mentors. Mentors generally come in the way of older, wealthier, and more experienced individuals who are willing to share their knowledge with you. The great thing about having a mentor, or mentors, is that they can help you through their own experience. They can teach you about how they made their money. Most importantly, this is a real person that you can look up to. Sure, you might admire Bill Gates, Warren Buffet, or Jeff Bezos, but the fact is that having someone you can actually talk to helps keep you grounded.

On the whole, the mentor's role is to help you discover your own path. Naturally, your job is not to copy your mentor's plan. After all, that plan was successful for them. If they are much older than you, they made their money in a very different kind of economy. As such, you might not necessarily be playing in the same circumstances. Nevertheless, they did things right. These are the things which you need to learn from.

For instance, your mentor surely was responsible for their finances, dedicated to their craft, and astute at recognizing opportunity. These are traits that you can emulate during your personal journey toward success. Moreover, a mentor can help you stay focused, especially during the tough times. Mentors often share their personal stories as a means of teaching valuable skills. These are the kind of real-life skills that are hard to teach in a business school. Unless you have the opportunity to study with highly experienced and knowledgeable professors, it would be quite difficult to learn valuable life skills from a textbook.

Another interesting characteristic of successful investors is that they study history. The best investors are historians. Now, please don't think that we are going to discuss the ancient Roman Empire. By "history," we're talking about how business has evolved. This means that it's important to study what made the great business leaders of the past success. It's also vitally important to study how and why the wealthy made their money. When you study these great leaders, you will find that they all have common traits.

A great place to start is the magnum opus penned by Napoleon Hill, "Think and Grow Rich." This is a timeless piece that focuses on the great leaders of industry from the early 20th century. The business leaders and influential individuals who served as fodder for this book made their money through their own hard work and dedication. The vast majority of them were self-made millionaires, who in many cases, were immigrants who made their lives in the United States. Sure, the circumstances in which these folks made their money was quite different then. But the core principles still hold true today.

Another great book that you ought to check out is "The Millionaire Next Door" by Stanley and Danko. This book was born out of PhD-level research conducted on America's wealthiest individuals. To the surprise of the authors, the wealthiest households in the United States featured average citizens who worked hard and saved their money. Then, they invested carefully while avoiding the usual traps that set most people back. The lessons that are distilled in this book make for a fascinating read. So, it's definitely worth checking out so that you can further your understanding of the way you can make money.

Ultimately, making money is not about inheriting a vast fortune or getting lucky with a million-dollar idea. The secret to building wealth is about knowing who you are, what you want, and where you want to go. With this knowledge, you can then go about acquiring the assets you need you to make this life come true. Before you know it, you will be well on your way to making your dreams a reality.

Looking Toward the Future of Investing

The old saying "the future is now" is perfectly apropos in this case. The future is already here in terms of how the internet and computer technology has enabled us to automate much of the manual tasks that we once used to do. For example, the use of e-banking has greatly facilitated many of the financial transactions that we once did. Now, you don't have to stand in line to pay your bills. All you need to do is log on to your e-banking software, and you are good to go.

A great example of how modern technology has enabled the average person to get in on the action is day trading. Through day trading, you can take control of your investment activity. You can play the role of stockbroker right from your personal computer. This is a rather straightforward way in which you can cut out the middleman and make your own investment decisions. Win or lose; you have the control to choose when you invest. You can choose your preferred instruments while also making the most of the various opportunities the market provides you.

Another great example of taking control of your own destiny is crypto investing. Since the crypto market is, be definition digital, you don't need to rely on a third-party broker to make decisions for you. You can decide when you jump into the action and when you can cash out. The great thing about it is that once you learn the ropes, you won't have to pay hefty commissions or upfront membership fees. In fact, you can build a steady source of income that no one can ever take away from you.

On the whole, the future of investing is set on the internet. If you aren't totally proficient with online investment tools, then it's time to do a little more research into the tools that you can use to your benefit. At the end of the day, making the most of digital investment tools can help you get one step closer to your objectives and desired outcomes.

Lastly, always keep an open mind. One of the cardinal sins of investing is not keeping an open mind. When your mindset becomes restricted to a single type of investment, then you won't be able to keep up with the times. There will come a point in which the trends of the market will either knock you out of the game or severely limit your ability to make money. Think about all of those stockbrokers who refused to embrace computers back in the 1980s. They still relied on typewriters and telephones to make trades.

Nowadays, that seems like ancient history. In particular, algorithmic trading has made stockbrokers' jobs far simpler than ever.

So, it's vitally important for you to keep an open mind at all times. You never know when the next big thing might come along. By keeping an open mind, you will be able to get in on it in the early going, that is, at the stage when everyone makes real money.

The Name of the Game Is "Flexibility"

Speaking of being open-minded, successful investors are always flexible. This means that you need to be willing to alter your investment strategy to suit the pace of the game. For instance, let's assume you are fully invested in stocks. Then, there is a sharp market downturn. Thanks to your careful planning, you recognized the situation well before any serious damage came to your portfolio. At this point, you decided to alter the allocation of your investment portfolio so that you reduce your exposure to stocks and focus more on other types of investments, such as commodities and bonds.

This is what the pros do. They see trouble ahead and make the necessary adjustments. That way, by the time the majority of investors react, the pros are already out of harm's way. That is not a superpower that you gain by way of a freak nuclear accident. This is the type of skill that you can learn from experience and study. In the best of cases, you are able to acquire these skills from your study of history. You can recognize the warning signs and make adjustments accordingly.

Additionally, being flexible is also about recognizing when a strategy isn't working. There is nothing wrong with admitting that something didn't go as expected. If anything, it's foolish to cling to a strategy that is failing just because you're too proud to admit it didn't work.

The fact of the matter is that being able to accept your mistakes and learn from them, is a skill that highly successful investors develop early on. Yes, it sucks to be wrong. It's even worse to lose money in the process. However, it's far worse to go down with the ship just because you are too stubborn to admit it's sinking.

Yes, even legendary investors make mistakes. They misjudge the potential of a company or misread the signs in the market. Yes, the experts lose money, too. But what separates the good investors from the elite is that they are quick to put failures behind them and look to the future. This is an important trait that you need to keep in mind. If you dwell on past mistakes for too long, the only thing you are going to be doing is undermining your own confidence. When your confidence begins to dwindle, so will your motivation. Sadly, folks who let their failures get to them, end up cashing out their investments and blowing the money.

In the end, achieving your desired outcomes is a road that you need to follow, especially when times are tough. Naturally, flexibility means that you may have to take a detour from time to time. But that doesn't mean that you should quit everything and tear the whole plan down. Even the best investors hit significant bumps along the way. What sets them apart from the wannabes is the fact that they have a vision they are committed to. It's this vision that allows them to get through the lean times.

So, the next time you close your eyes, visualize what you want your life to be. When you see exactly what you want, make a promise to yourself that you will do everything you can to make it happen. Will it be easy? Most likely, no. But it will definitely be worth it once you get there.

Conclusion

Thank you very much for taking the time to read this book. We hope it has been insightful and has provided you with the information you need to get started in the world of investing. Whether you are just starting out or whether you are looking to further your understanding, we are sure that you have found something to help you on your road to successful investing.

So, what's next?

If you haven't already done so, it's time to do some homework. We highly encourage you to look into the various types of investments you can engage in right away. These investments may be something as simple as opening a high-yield savings account. You may also look to take some money you have saved up for a rainy day and put it into a CD. In other cases, you may even look into a mutual fund or even bonds.

If you are keen on getting your feet wet in the stock market, there are plenty of ways in which you can gain exposure. Best of all, you don't need to start out with a huge sum of money. Even a small investment can pay off in the long run. All you need is to make the decision to get started.

This is exactly where it all begins. When you make the decision to become an investor and stop being a consumer, you will find that all sorts of opportunities become available to you. The world no longer seems like a struggle. Sure, life won't get any easier, but you won't have your mindset dragging you down. You'll have the motivation and the attitude needed to keep you afloat, especially when things are getting you down.

Please bear in mind that making it in the investment world is a combination of knowledge and perseverance. Those who lack the patience to see their investment plan through often come up short when they need it most. However, if you are willing to see your investment plan through, you'll find that your life will eventually turn out to be everything you want it to be. While it may not be easy to get there, you will have everything you've ever wanted at the end of the day. In fact, you'll be surprised to find that you have so much more than you could have ever hoped for.

Thank you once again for taking the time to read this book. If you have found it to be useful and informative in any way, please tell your friends, family, colleagues, or anyone you think would benefit from the information contained herein. We hope that they too, will find the inspiration you have to transform their lives.

The time has come to stop thinking about "what if" and start focusing on everything you could do to make it better. Good luck and happy investing!

Printed in Great Britain
by Amazon